THE EL

M000042929

Preparing for the Double Portion

Michael B. French

THE ELISHA WAY is a radical, innovative and inspiring approach to discipleship. Michael's insightful melding of the need for fathers to want to be fathers and the need for sons to want to be sons - if followed - would revolutionize the Body of Christ.

— **John Paul Jackson**
Streams Ministries International

This book is like a blueprint that would guide us in to that prophetic model and would place us in the land of our inheritance and appropriation of our covenant blessings. I cannot think of a more vital subject to be addressed by God's people nor a more valuable tool to facilitate that journey than THE ELISHA WAY.

— **Paul Keith Davis**
WhiteDove Ministries

Michael French's book THE ELISHA WAY will be a great tool in this time of transition, moving this generation to the next new level. It is imperative that we grasp the key of "Son-ship"! I recommend this book without hesitation; your spiritual life will be enriched.

— **Bobby Conner**
EaglesView Ministries

THE ELISHA WAY... Pastor Michael French has written a needful and wonderfully timely, prophetic book revealing the true spirit and value of Sonship. Elisha was a true son to Elijah. Their relationship revealed the kingdom's mandate and benefit of calling The Fathers to the Sons and the Sons to the Father for intimate relationship and training. This book is a must-read for all Christian leaders and believers.

— **Joe Brock**
Cutting Edge Ministries Church
President of Advocate Ministries, Inc.

I highly recommend THE ELISHA WAY: *Preparing for the Double Portion.* Michael French points to a balanced diet for the church to walk in when it deals with spiritual sons and fathers. It speaks of a clarion call to the Elisha's and Elijah's in this generation to arise from their state of slumber and walk as the mentors and leaders God has called them to be. If you're looking for a good book to teach you how to be responsible, dedicated to the call, and make the shift to be a foundational piece while others are on shaky ground, this book is for you.

— Jeremy Lopez
Identity Network, Inc.

Pastor Michael French has given us a well written, easy reading, totally biblical examination of the relationship of spiritual father/mother and son/daughter. The author calls elders in the church today to live a deep spiritual life in Christ so that God can use them to encourage, teach, protect, inspire, and pray for newer Christians. He challenges the younger in Christ to share life and ministry with an elder "as a son with his father". How great will be the fruits of the Spirit in the souls and in the communities of Christians if we heed Pastor French's message!

— Dr. William Wilson
Assisting Bishop
Anglican Diocese of the South

In this season of tremendous Global challenge, many people seem to believe that they are destined for failure. It is refreshing to see a book that calls for Fathers to arise and release a double portion. This book is right on time. The author uses his heart of a pastor, his mind of a scholar, and his communication skills of a lawyer to point people to a pathway of freedom and hope. This is not only Elisha's way for a double portion, but God's way as well. It is a must-read for all.

— Dr. "Steve" Kabachia Munyiri
Founder of Agape Fellowship
Nairobi, Kenya

THE ELISHA WAY

Preparing for the Double Portion

Michael B. French

Foreword by Paul Keith Davis
Cover design by Christos Georghiou

ISBN: 978-1-937331-00-9
Copyright @ 2011 ShadeTree Publishing, LLC
1038 N. Eisenhower Dr. #274
Beckley, West Virginia 25801

Visit our Web site at www.ShadeTreePublishing.com

TABLE OF CONTENTS

DEDICATION

This book is dedicated, first and foremost, to the Lord God of Elijah. May his face be seen in the earth once again as it was in the days of Elijah. It is also dedicated to the Elisha generation, and as such to my sons, Joshua, Caleb, Jacob, and Noah. May they truly take up the mantle that God has destined for them and receive the double portion as their inheritance.

FOREWORD
by Paul Keith Davis, WhiteDove Ministries

"Our Father which art in heaven." Those are the initial words to the prophetic model for prayer that the Lord Jesus gave when He walked the earth in human form. God's biblical model from the outset of history has always been that of fathers and sons. Although we have lost much of that perspective throughout Church history, we are entering a season of profound restoration that will return us to the God ordained ideals for leadership and relationship.

Clearly, the days in which we live are saturated with prophetic significance and promise. The Bible abundantly speaks of the "Last Days" and the profound grace that will be demonstrated to produce the mature "sons of God" who all of creation is groaning to see. For there to be sons, there must also be spiritual fathers who bless them. It has been my observation in recent years that vast numbers of ministers are looking for fatherly relationships that provide covering, mentoring, and encouragement. THE ELISHA WAY will be a valuable tool to launch us in to that objective.

In the many years that I have known Michael French, he has always demonstrated a keen sensitivity to the prophetic gospel and a sense of scholarship that presents truth in clear and palatable ways. THE ELISHA WAY is a perfect example of that gifting. This book comes at a kairos moment in human history that will strike a chord within the radical remnant seeking to encounter God in profound and experiential ways and function in God's promise as the mature sons.

Michael very astutely outlines the need for us to return to the Hebraic model of leadership, which has always been that of fathers and sons. God Himself was a Father to Abraham and blessed him with covenant blessings. That privilege was bestowed to Isaac who then released it to Jacob. This impartation is very closely akin to the apostolic blessing that is to be released in our day between fathers and sons, launching them into personal and corporate destiny with not only a good biblical foundation, but also a father's blessing.

At the beginning of our ministry, the Lord commissioned us to create a culture of honor as it relates to the prior generations and the anointed ministries that paved the way as pioneers and prototypes. As a result, we have highlighted numerous "fathers" of the prior generation with an emphasis on the great contributions they provided and the breakthrough anointings demonstrated in their ministries. Although we do not turn a blinded eye to weaknesses and mistakes, we also approached them from a posture of learning so that we do not make similar mistakes in our generation. The Lord has said by creating a culture of honor, the blessings of those fathers, or as we have often said mantles that they carried, will be released upon the sons in our generation.

One of the most often quoted passages concerning the passing of an anointing is 2 Kings 2:9-14, the transference of the mantle of God's Spirit from Elijah to Elisha. The relationship between these two prophets contains valuable principles with 21st-century relevance. Throughout THE ELISHA WAY, we find many inspired insights that will help position us for profound blessing and activation of our last day calling as sons, Disciples of Christ and the friends of God.

The apostle Paul acknowledged that we have many teachers but very few fathers. A teacher imparts information; yet a father releases spiritual blessings that awaken gifts, callings, and prophetic destiny. This and more are covered in depth through THE ELISHA WAY with both biblical examples and present-day relevance.

Much of the church today is structured with businesslike models that streamline people through programs and institutions. Even so, in the midst of all the instruction, a remnant of people will return to the true model of fathers/sons that produces great fruitfulness and spiritual maturity. Michael provides profound insights that will transition us into that flow. Those who read this book will discover keys to unlock spiritual doors and reveal God's heart for this generation and His people.

The heart of the Father is demonstrated through spiritual fathers providing instruction, spiritual guidance, protection, correction, and inspiration to go higher. Michael offers great strategies for fathers who are willing to provide these valuable ingredients and sons who are willing to receive them.

For many years, we have been prophesying "new things." The time has now come for words to meet actions. This book is like a blueprint that would guide us in to that prophetic model and would place us in the land of our inheritance and appropriation of our covenant blessings. I cannot think of a more vital subject to be addressed by God's people nor a more valuable tool to facilitate that journey than THE ELISHA WAY.

INTRODUCTION

The topic of discipleship is critical for the church today. For too long, we have been seeking to produce converts at the expense of producing disciples. In fact, our effort to grow the church has created a seeker-sensitive culture that tends to paint Christianity as a come-to-Jesus-and-all-your-problems-will-be-solved religion, or a let's-not-offend-anyone-so-they-will-join-our-church culture. These warped perspectives of faith cannot endure alongside a strong emphasis on true, biblical discipleship, thus referred to as "sonship". While issues are certain to arise over the coexistence of contemporary, post-modern views on church and the clarion call to establish spiritual Father/Son relationships in the church, I am confident that the call to true discipleship must triumph.

Malachi makes a strong declaration that in the last days, the hearts of the fathers must be turned back to the children, and the hearts of the children must be turned back to the fathers (Malachi 4:5-6). This book assumes that we are living in the last of the last days (after all, Jesus told his disciples that they were living in the last days 2000 years ago). Therefore, it is time for the cry of Malachi to be fulfilled.

As both a pastor and an author, I recognize the significance of the ideas conveyed in this book. I also recognize that most of my references and examples are couched the masculine gender. It is my heartfelt desire to convey the significance of men fulfilling their destiny and truly becoming spiritual fathers, but I am aware that women have an equally vital role to play in the establishment of the Kingdom. As a result, it is my desire that those who read these pages would not be confused by the use of masculine gender and led to believe that this book is only for men. Feel free to substitute mother and daughter for father and son as you read.

In the end, it is as essential that the church become as much a place filled with spiritual parents who are raising godly, spiritual children as it is a place filled with natural parents who are raising godly, natural children. In the US culture today, young men and women are departing from the faith as they reach young adulthood, and few of them ever return. When the author of Proverbs wrote, "Train up a child in the way he should go, and when he is old he will not depart from it" (Proverbs 22:6), I believe that those words were intended for both natural and spiritual parents. We must take up the call and become spiritual parents to an Elisha generation, so that we may see them cease their departure from the paths of righteousness and instead grow to greater heights of maturity that will usher in the Kingdom of Heaven for a desperate world to find.

Chapter 1
RESTORING SONSHIP

Today's society hungers for power. Men and women, old and young, diligently seek to harness it. The quest to obtain real spiritual authority has taken the populace down numerous pathways. These paths have included New Age Spirituality, Wicca, Paganism, Islam, Hinduism, Buddhism, Taoism, and many more. However, rarely does our culture look to Christianity for the source of the reality it seeks. Christianity is relegated to a second-class religion claiming to have all the answers, but offering no proof of its relevance.

Relevance of Christianity

We've lost the ability to pass the strength of our faith to the next generation; consequently, Christianity has been slipping towards a loss of our cultural relevance. With each passing of the torch, the cultural significance of Christianity grows dimmer, and thus society loses sight. With the light of the Gospel becoming so dim, it has become necessary for us to re-evaluate where we stand as Christians.

Despite the many attempts by the church to regain its former relevance, it often seems we are

3

fighting a losing battle. According to the research conducted by Josh McDowell's ministry, 81% of Christian youth no longer believe in the concept of absolute truth.[1] When we reluctantly acknowledge that this research assessed Christian youth, we find the results shocking. The very existence of such evidence should sound an alarm for change. Josh McDowell said, "today merely 'believing' isn't enough. Not because believing isn't important; it is. But, in today's culture believing is made out to be more of a preference based on one's subjective feelings at the moment. And that kind of believing isn't enough".[2]

Although many methods have been attempted to bring about change (one of the most prominent being the use of the seeker-sensitive model of church), few have been successful in reclaiming lost ground. Unfortunately, many seeker-sensitive techniques have unwittingly abandoned the heart of Christianity in favor of regaining societal acceptance. (Please note that this statement is in no way intended to indicate that all seeker-sensitive models have failed. There are certainly some that have been successful in fulfilling their biblical mandate.)

---

[1] Josh McDowell and Bob Hostetler, *Beyond Belief to Convictions* (Wheaton, Illinois: Tyndale House, 2002), 12.

[2]Ibid., 21.

In its efforts to reach the unbeliever, the seeker-sensitive model for reaching the lost sometimes begins to look more like those they are trying to reach, rather than teaching them to look like Christ. Thus, all too often, these ministries have become more in the world and of it, rather than in the world and not of it. In order for the church to regain its cultural relevance, we must do more than entertain the population in an effort to bolster our numbers. We must restore the value of the absolute truth embodied by Christ's statement that He alone is The Way, The Truth, and The Life (John 14:6). While the world demands that the church change in order to prove its relevance, the true mission of the church is to become the light of the world (Matthew 5:14) that shines uncompromisingly. It is only in this way that we can transform a generation for whom believing is not enough.

It is time to find a new model. However, Ecclesiastes 1:9 tells us that there is nothing new under the sun. According to the wisdom of this passage, we are actually not looking for a new model, but rather, we must return to an ancient model set forth in the Word of God and illustrated in the lives of the men and women described therein. To restore relevance to the church, we must return to a Biblical model that allows the torch to be passed while seeing an increase in the light with each passing.

With the admonitions of the Ecclesiastical writer taken to heart, we can turn back the pages of time and ask ourselves how faith remained relevant in other trying times. The Bible describes one such difficult time as the period in Israel's history when Ahab and Jezebel ruled. (Even to this day, the name Jezebel is associated with demonic attack and the usurping of true spiritual authority.) This was also the time when Elijah, one of the greatest prophets of the Bible, found himself questioning his ability to continue and God's ability to preserve the truth (1 Kings 19:1-14). In these ancient writings, we can find answers to the same questions we're facing today.

The Elisha Model

The relationship between Elijah and his protégé Elisha paints of vivid picture of the proper transference and increase of spiritual authority, even when surrounded by a hostile society. The book of 1Kings recounts how Elisha was called.

> *So he departed from there, and found Elisha the son of Shaphat, who was plowing with twelve yoke of oxen before him, and he was with the twelfth. Then Elijah passed by him and threw his mantle on him. And he left the oxen and ran after Elijah, and said," Please let me kiss my father and my mother, and then I will follow you."*
> *-1 Kings 19:19-20 NKJV*

In the face of a hostile environment, Elijah finds Elisha consumed with the business of the day, yet ready and willing to take up the challenge of living a life of faith Not only does Elisha ultimately maintain the zeal, power, and authority of Elijah within the culture of his day, but ultimately he walks in a double portion of that spirit and anointing.

And so it was, when they had crossed over, that Elijah said to Elisha, "Ask! What may I do for you, before I am taken away from you? "Elisha said, "Please let a double portion of your spirit be upon me. "So he said, "You have asked a hard thing. Nevertheless, if you see me when I am taken from you, it shall be so for you; but if not, it shall not be so." Then it happened, as they continued on and talked, that suddenly a chariot of fire appeared with horses of fire, and separated the two of them; and Elijah went up by a whirlwind into heaven. And Elisha saw it, and he cried out," My father, my father, the chariot of Israel and its horsemen!" So he saw him no more. And he took hold of his own clothes and tore them into two pieces. He also took up the mantle of Elijah that had fallen from him, and went back and stood by the bank of the Jordan. Then he took the mantle of Elijah that had fallen from him, and struck the water, and said, "Where is the LORD God of Elijah?" And when he also

had struck the water, it was divided this
way and that; and Elisha crossed over.
-2 Kings 2:9-14 NKJV

A careful examination of this relationship can help us to better understand how to handle the challenges to our faith. If Elijah can train and equip Elisha in the face of Jezebel and all of the false religious philosophies of his day, then certainly the principles he used will still be effective today.

Our current methods and models are weakening the church, yet when faced with equal challenges. Elisha walked away with a double portion of the spirit of Elijah. When we recognize this, we must also acknowledge the need to embrace the Elisha Way of being equipped. We live in the midst of a generation that is hungry for spiritual power and authority. This is a generation that will not be satisfied with business as usual. We face a day where there are only two possibilities: either young men and women must become an Elisha Generation, <u>or</u> they will be lost.

True Discipleship

While it is appropriate to call the connection between Elijah and Elisha a discipleship relationship, it is also awkward. The perceived value of discipleship has waxed and waned over the years. Discipleship has been espoused as the key to the Christian life by some, and has been denounced as a form of slavery by others. (In the past, discipleship programs have run the gamut from glorified Bible studies to oppressive relationships that seemed far more like master/servant than mentor/student.) Regardless of our personal perceptions of discipleship, the mentoring relationship of Elijah and Elisha (as well as Jesus and his followers) is the real key to the restoration of spiritual power and the true relevance of the church. It is the training ground for true spiritual sons and daughters.

In truth, the lack of genuine discipleship has contributed highly to the lack of relevance of the church and to the generational abandonment of the acceptance of absolute truth. When the church loses the ability to effectively pass the torch (or to pass the mantle as it can be referred to in the context of the Elijah/Elisha relationship), it results in the very situation that we face today – a world filled with seekers, searching in all the wrong places for an answer that they will not believe to be found within the doors of the church. Perhaps this is true because the Gospel was never meant to be contained within the walls of the church, but rather openly presented as a part of the daily routine of Christians.

When the spiritual authority carried by each passing generation diminishes rather than increases, it is time to dig deep, leave no stone unturned, and examine the core of our belief systems. If we are to truly restore the father/son discipleship model demonstrated by Elijah and Elisha, then it is essential that we be honest with ourselves. The starting point for such an examination may seem strange to many, yet in fact, it lies in the very terminology we use to distinguish ourselves from the rest of the world's religions. Those who have accepted the free gift of everlasting life (by means of believing with their heart and confessing with their mouth that the resurrected Son of God is both our Savior and Lord (Romans 10:9)) have taken upon themselves the name of "Christian". In order to fully embrace the Elisha Way of being equipped, we must first consider exactly what this designation means.

The word Christian is the English translation of the Greek word *Christianos* (khris-tee-an-os'), which means to be a follower of Christ.[3] This seems, at first glance, to be an acceptable designation for those that might otherwise be identified by church terminology as born again. Do we dare to look closer? When we are honest with ourselves, we must question whether or not we are even worthy of bearing this title at all. (It should be recognized that the preceding sentence is used as much for its shock value as for any other reason; however, it is a legitimate question.) This question is in not intended to challenge anyone's salvation only to challenge our commitment.

_____

[3]Biblesoft's New Exhaustive Strong's Numbers and Concordance with Expanded Greek-Hebrew Dictionary. Copyright (c) 1994, Biblesoft and International Bible Translators, Inc.

Most people would agree that the gift of eternal life is available to all who believe; however, there must be something more to what it means to be a Christian. All those who have ever played the game of Monopoly are familiar with the get-out-of-jail-free card. Unfortunately, many of those who have been saved consider it nothing more than having drawn a get-out-of-hell-free card from the deck of life. This ought not to be so! While few would question that those who have received salvation in this manner have equal access to the gift of everlasting life, the question of whether or not they should bear the name of Christian can and should be asked. There must be something more to being a true follower of Christ.

Is it possible that we have missed the mark? If the term Christian means to be a follower of Christ, then the use of that term implies that we are successfully doing it. If we are effective Christians, then where are the signs that are supposed to follow us (Mark 16:17-18), and where are the greater works that Jesus said we should be doing (John 14:12)?

Perhaps we are not as successful at being Christians as we think we are. When New Testament terminology is considered in connection with this question, it must be remembered that it was far more frequent to refer to those who had accepted the Gospel as disciples than it was to refer to them as Christians. In fact, the word Christian is used only three times in the entire New Testament with the first time being found in Acts 11.

> *Then Barnabas departed for Tarsus to seek*
> *Saul. And when he had found him, he*
> *brought him to Antioch. So it was that for a*
> *whole year they assembled with the church*
> *and taught a great many people. And the*
> *disciples were first called Christians in*
> *Antioch.*
>
> -Acts 11:25-26 NKJV

The word disciple is an English translation of the Greek word *mathetes* (math-ay-tes'), which means learner[4] or a person who learns from others by either formal or informal instruction.[5]

It can be argued that the reason we have such difficulty in passing the mantle in our society is that we have made too many converts. Without proper opportunity to learn, these converts have simply assumed themselves to be Christians. If we cannot in good conscience claim to be successfully following the pattern that Jesus left for us to follow, then our focus must return to becoming better students. This understanding of discipleship's definition and meaning can radically change our ability to pass the mantle, as well as increase the relevance of the local church in

---

[4]Biblesoft's New Exhaustive Strong's Numbers and Concordance with Expanded Greek-Hebrew Dictionary. Copyright (c) 1994, Biblesoft and International Bible Translators, Inc.

[5]Greek-English Lexicon Based on Semantic Domain. Copyright (c) 1988 United Bible Societies, New York.

our culture. Likewise, the failure to embrace an understanding of these biblical principles can be seen as a failure to embrace the Elisha Way.

Just as we can examine the success of the Elijah/Elisha relationship to encourage us in our appreciation of true discipleship, we can examine the lives of the disciples as seen in the early church to begin to understand the results of such discipleship. When the number of disciples (i.e., learners) multiplied in the early church, so did the number who came to the faith.

> *Now in those days, when the number of the disciples was multiplying, there arose a complaint against the Hebrews by the Hellenists, because their widows were neglected in the daily distribution. Then the twelve summoned the multitude of the disciples and said, "It is not desirable that we should leave the word of God and serve tables. Therefore, brethren, seek out from among you seven men of good reputation, full of the Holy Spirit and wisdom, whom we may appoint over this business; but we will give ourselves continually to prayer and to the ministry of the word." And the saying pleased the whole multitude. And they chose Stephen, a man full of faith and the Holy Spirit, and Philip, Prochorus, Nicanor, Timon, Parmenas, and Nicolas, a proselyte from Antioch, whom they set before the apostles; and when they had prayed, they laid hands on them. Then the*

Apostles

word of God spread, and the number of the disciples multiplied greatly in Jerusalem, and a great many of the priests were obedient to the faith.

-Acts 6:1-7 NKJV

The first verse states that the number of disciples (or learners) was increasing, and as a result, an issue over the disciples' roles arose. The disciples arranged for the more mature ones to mentor the younger ones, so that the best equipped could focus on equipping. The passage goes on to say that the word of God spread, more disciples were made, and many priests became obedient to the faith. If we are not careful, the significance of this last statement can be easily missed. To fully understand, we must remember who the priests were.

The priests were sacred men who were the religious leaders of the day. They were self-proclaimed seekers of the truth, but in reality, they had simply become very religious. For all their gained religion, they had lost their relationship and did not recognize Truth (that is Jesus) when it arrived. When the early church began to focus on discipleship by allowing the twelve to focus on the word of God and equipping others, the number of individuals finding truth increased. As a result, the priests were drawn to re-examine their own beliefs. In doing so, many priests left their emphasis on religion, returned to relationship and were transformed. Just like for the priests, when confronted by real truth in a real way that is relevant, our lives will be transformed too.

Today, there is a generation of young people going about their business and desiring something more. If we are serious about our desire to see society find a reason to embrace the truth that we hold dear, then we must return to our roots and once again become disciples of the Word. This present day Elisha generation can glean a double portion of what we have, but only if we will again embrace our role as equippers of the saints and as real Christians.

This book will challenge us as Christians to become Elijahs and Elishas of these latter days. In doing so we will be forced to recognize that, it's not about putting a new face on an old idea, but rather about embracing an ancient concept in a way that has never lost its relevance. We must become successful students if we are ever to become successful followers. If we desire for Jesus to be seen in us and through us, then the Elisha Way is the only way. Relationship is the key to all that we believe. Rituals, habits, patterns, and programs (though unquestionably beneficial at times) will never make us who we want to be, but relationship can change our lives.

Paul once said, "Imitate me as I imitate Christ" (1 Corinthians 11:1). This passage implied that Paul wanted others to study him as he followed Christ, in order that by mimicking him, they might also learn to follow Christ more closely for themselves. This is not so surprising when we consider that the simplest way a child learns is through imitation, particularly the imitation of a parent. We are in need of students who will imitate Christ and become spiritual fathers whom we can imitate as children. We are in need of fathers like Elijah and sons like Elisha. We are in desperate need of the restoration of true relationships that will return relevance to the term sonship.

Chapter 2
LIKE FATHER LIKE SON

yr need to
R→focus

The heart of discipleship is found not in the training and equipping, but rather in the relationships forged along the way. Religion places an emphasis upon the form and process, while relationship places an emphasis upon the individual. True discipleship is, at its core, based upon the development of sincere, heart-felt relationships between individuals. It is through the formation of such relationships that real training and equipping actually take place. If we are willing to acknowledge this truth regarding discipleship, then it becomes essential that we also take time to examine the type of relationships that should be formed. If we form proper relationships, discipleship will be successful and for spiritual sons will be birthed. Once again, the relationship between Elijah and Elisha provides key insight into this question and demonstrates the basic components of a father/son relationship.

The Elijah Example

The relationship between Elijah and Elisha can be characterized in a number of ways (teacher/student; master/servant; or even friend/friend), but perhaps the most significant approach is unexpected. Although there is no indication that Elijah and Elisha had any form of blood relationship, the central relationship between them (at least as far as the process of discipleship is concerned) is one of father and son. Some might suggest that this is merely a symbolic relationship, the importance of which is based solely in the context of metaphor; however, I sincerely believe that it is much deeper and much more significant. In fact, based upon an examination of the Word of God it would appear that, at least on a spiritual basis, this father/son relationship has much greater impact than a natural blood relationship ever would. The clearest evidence of the existence of this type of relationship is found in the closing moments of their time together.

> *And Elisha saw it, and he cried out, "My father, my father, the chariot of Israel and its horsemen!" So he saw him no more. And he took hold of his own clothes and tore them into two pieces*
> Sign of grief
> -2 Kings 2:12 NKJV

In this passage, not only does Elisha cry out and call Elijah his father, but he does so in such a way as to place great emphasis upon the relationship itself. This double proclamation ("my father, my father") had far greater significance in the Near Eastern culture of that time than it does today. Within the confines of

18

our postmodern culture, we might view such a proclamation, particularly under the surrounding circumstances, as being nothing more than an excited utterance; however, when we consider the cultural context within which this statement was made, it is far more significant.

In the Semitic culture, calling a person's name (or in this case their title) twice was a method of showing the deepest of respect. It conveyed the idea of endearment, of a deep and personal friendship. By saying, "my father, my father", Elisha is actually conveying his love for Elijah and the fact that Elijah is dear to him. In our culture, we have difficulty understanding this kind of depth in relationships between those who are not related by blood or marriage.

Today, we use language loosely. In the cultural context of the passage, the words themselves were accompanied by heartfelt actions. Merely calling a person's name twice is no longer evidence of a deep and personal relationship. More likely, it is perceived as lip service. Even by the time of Christ, such a perception was not fully without merit, as Jesus warns against those who serve him merely by lip service by making reference to this very same cultural expression.

"Not everyone who says to Me, 'Lord, Lord,' shall enter the kingdom of heaven, but he who does the will of My Father in heaven.

> *Many will say to Me in that day, 'Lord,*
> *Lord, have we not prophesied in Your*
> *name, cast out demons in Your name, and*
> *done many wonders in Your name?' And*
> *then I will declare to them, 'I never knew*
> *you; depart from Me, you who practice*
> *lawlessness!'*
>
> -Matthew 7:21-23 NKJV

Notice the use of "Lord, Lord" in this context. Jesus is actually teaching that a person can't just say that they have a personal relationship with Him, but rather they must live their life as an expression of that relationship. Here Jesus says that those who speak with their mouth (without living with their life) are guilty of violating the law; they are practitioners of lawlessness. According to the book of Deuteronomy, a true, heartfelt relationship with God is based on obedience.

> *"See, I have set before you today life and*
> *good, death and evil, in that I command*
> *you today to love the LORD your God, to*
> *walk in His ways, and to keep His*
> *commandments, His statutes, and His*
> *judgments, that you may live and multiply;*
> *and the LORD your God will bless you in*
> *the land which you go to possess.*
>
> -Deuteronomy 30:15-17 NKJV

James admonishes us in the same manner when he warns that faith without works is dead (James 2:17). In other words, proclamations are empty without action. Words alone are not enough to

20

establish the deep level of a relationship required for real discipleship. In the life of Elisha, we find a lifestyle of action that confirms his father/son relationship with Elijah and illustrates the sincerity of his spoken "my father, my father".

> *And it came to pass, when the LORD was about to take up Elijah into heaven by a whirlwind, that Elijah went with Elisha from Gilgal. Then Elijah said to Elisha, "Stay here, please, for the LORD has sent me on to Bethel." But Elisha said, "As the LORD lives, and as your soul lives, I will not leave you!" So they went down to Bethel. Now the sons of the prophets who were at Bethel came out to Elisha, and said to him, "Do you know that the LORD will take away your master from over you today?" And he said, "Yes, I know; keep silent!" Then Elijah said to him, "Elisha, stay here, please, for the LORD has sent me on to Jericho." But he said, "As the LORD lives, and as your soul lives, I will not leave you!" So they came to Jericho. Now the sons of the prophets who were at Jericho came to Elisha and said to him, "Do you know that the LORD will take away your master from over you today?" So he answered, "Yes, I know; keep silent!" Then Elijah said to him, "Stay here, please, for the LORD has sent me on to the Jordan. "But he said, "As the LORD lives, and as*

*your soul lives, I will not leave you!" So the
two of them went on.*

-2 Kings 2:1-6, NKJV

Notice how diligently Elijah endeavors to convince Elisha not to follow him, and how persistently Elisha insists upon continuing to accompany his master, Elijah, on the journey. This is not the response of a student to a teacher, of a servant to his master, nor even of one friend to another, but rather it is the response of a son to his father.

Consider Elisha's refusal to leave the side of Elijah, even in the face of Elijah's repeated requests. What could motivate Elisha to take this course? What bolsters his confidence even in the face of Elijah's objections? It is the deep bonds of relationship forged between a parent and child, between a father and his son. It is only natural that Elijah, recognizing that the time of his departure has arrived, yet not knowing in what form it would be completed, would prefer that his son not see the moment of his death. On the other hand, it is equally natural that Elisha, also recognizing that Elijah's departure is imminent, would refuse to leave his father in those final hours.

Having established that the relationship between these two is more akin to that of a father and son than any other, the question now becomes: what does this mean and what can it teach us about the road toward becoming a part of this Elisha generation? In order for us to understand how such relationships enhance the discipleship process, these questions must be

22

answered. To answer these questions, we must further examine the basics of the father/son relationship. While there are certainly many aspects to the relationship between fathers and sons, the heart of such relationships is composed of four basic components: affection, devotion, imitation, and separation.

Affection

The first and most significant of the components that distinguish the father/son relationship can be found in the deep and abiding love that exists between a father and his son. It is this love that allows the relationship to be tested and bent, but to remain unbroken even through the most trying of times. Furthermore, this love allows the father/son relationship to endure, even when opinions differ and methods clash.

We must consider that Paul had a father/son relationship with the churches to whom he wrote. Paul had actually labored to give birth to these churches and in his life, we can see the example of a parental relationship with those churches he delivered and discipled. In his letter to the church at Philippi, Paul expressed that affection for his spiritual children was born out of the nature of Jesus Himself.

> *For God is my witness, how greatly I long*
> *for you all with the affection of Jesus*
> *Christ.*
>
> -Philippians 1:8, NKJV

This is the same kind of affection that is shown when Elisha lifts up the cry of his heart and proclaims, "my father, my father". It is the keystone mark of a father/son relationship.

Just as loving affection is the mark of strong natural relationships within earthly families; it is also the mark of strong discipleship relationships between spiritual fathers and sons. Many times in our culture, we think only of love and affection within the context of family ties or emotional bonds, never stopping to realize that loving and being loved by God through those around us is equally valuable. Jesus said, "These things I command you that you love one another"(Matthew 5:17).

This aspect of the father/son relationship has been under significant attack as society embraces the notion that affection between two men is a sign of homosexuality. The enemy uses the agenda of the radical homosexual community and the acceptance of an alternative lifestyle to not only promote sexual immorality, but also to target and taint this hallmark of the father/son relationship.

Affection is defined as "a tender feeling toward another; or fondness".[6] Years of lax moral standards and uncontested education concerning the homosexual lifestyle has left any such fondness between men in a state of confusion. We can no longer allow Satan to set the tone and define what it means to be a man, what it means to be a father, and most importantly, what it means to be a spiritual father.

Devotion

Fathers and sons should be devoted to each other, yet the concept of devotion seems to be lost on our modern culture. Devotion is defined as "ardent, often selfless affection and dedication, as to a person or principle".[7] Devotion goes beyond feelings and expresses itself in actions. For generations fathers instilled such dedication into their sons, however, today we see far too many latch key kids and single parent households for such devotion to be as visible as it should be.

---

[6]*The American Heritage® Dictionary of the English Language,* Fourth Edition Copyright © 2000 by Houghton Mifflin Company.Published by Houghton Mifflin Company. All rights reserved.

[7] Ibid.

The Biblical example of a father is one who gives of all that they are to sow into the life of their child in order to see that child succeed. The Biblical example of a son is one who honors the father and places value on what can be gleaned from their life. Both of these Biblical principles require an expression of self-sacrifice that is often lacking in our current culture, but can still be found if we search for it. When such devotion is missing from the natural parent-child relationship, it can and should still be found in the spiritual relationship. As this component of the spiritual father-son relationship is restored, it will also re-emerge in the natural relationship.

In a true father/son relationship, selfless devotion is based on love and trust. If the trust is violated, it becomes much more difficult for the love to endure alone. Violations of trust occur when the father figure misuses the son's devotion in order to dominate them. Subjugation is "to bring under control; conquer" or "to make subservient, enslave".[8] The abuse of devotion (resulting in subjugation) has hindered the proper role of discipleship in the church. Examples of such abuse were demonstrated to varying degrees by both the Shepherding Movement (or the Discipleship Movement, as it was also known) and by the People's Temple cult (founded and led by Jim

---

[8] Ibid.

26

Jones) in which individuals slipped across the line of Biblical teaching into undue influence and control.

Elijah didn't demand that Elisha serve him. Yet, after Elijah's death, Elisha was still referred to as the one who "poured water on the hands of Elijah"(2 Kings 3:11). Elisha served Elijah not because he felt pressured by Elijah, but out of devotion to Elijah and more importantly to the God of Elijah. When Elijah called Elisha, there was no mandate that required Elisha to follow. In fact, when Elisha asked to go and see his parents, Elijah responded with, "what have I done to you"(1 Kings 19:20) or in other words, "it is not me calling you and you have a choice as to whether or not to answer".

Only God has the right to demand our devotion, and yet he merely requests it.

> *I beseech you therefore, brethren, by the mercies of God, that you present your bodies a living sacrifice, holy, acceptable to God, which is your reasonable service.*
> -Romans 12:1-2, NKJV

Jesus used this same model when he chose His disciples. He merely called out "Follow me" (Mathew 4:19) and then it was up to them to make a decision. In this model, Jesus never demanded that His disciples follow Him; instead, they made the choice to follow him. It was never beyond God's power to make us serve Him, but He desired a people devoted to Him and not in bondage to Him. Devotion can only be given; it can never be demanded. We need a generation of spiritual fathers who give of their lives in order to see their spiritual sons succeed and a generation of spiritual sons who in turn give honor to those who equip them for the future.

Imitation

We often hear that imitation is the sincerest form of flattery. Flattery or not, imitation is a significant component of the father/son relationship. Children tend to exhibit the same patterns seen in the lives of their parents. Unfortunately, this frequently has both positive and negative consequences. The Word of God admonishes us to be careful in our choices of those whom we will imitate.

> *And we desire that each one of you show the same diligence to the full assurance of hope until the end, that you do not become sluggish, but imitate those who through faith and patience inherit the promises.*
> -Hebrews 6:11-12, NKJV

Who is worthy of imitation? Those who have endured to inherit the promises. Proverbs 20:21 reminds us that an inheritance hastily gained will not be blessed by God in the end. If we are to follow the example of someone as a part of the sonship process, then we must exercise great care in the choices that we make and we should be careful to consider whether or not they have stood the test of time. In addition, when we apply the concept of imitation to the process of becoming a spiritual son, we must keep another scriptural admonition in the forefront of our mind.

> *Therefore be imitators of God as dear children*
>
> -Ephesians 5:1, NKJV

For true discipleship to be effective, the concept of imitation must be embraced. However, first and foremost, we must always remember that we are to be imitators of Christ. Paul clearly indicated that it was acceptable to follow a spiritual father when he said, "Imitate me, just as I also imitate Christ" (1 Corinthians 11:1), but he also made it clear that imitating such a father was only valuable when our spiritual father is properly imitating Jesus.

Separation

Separation may seem an unlikely component of the father/son relationship; however, without it, the full purpose of sonship will not be recognized. Separation is inevitable in real life. A good son would never be expected to stay at home for the rest of his life. Instead, he is expected to learn life's lessons and then to step out and apply them in his own life. In fact, it's abnormal for this separation process to go unfulfilled; the Bible tells us to leave our father and mother to make our own life. The same is true with our spiritual parents.

Inevitably, the time came when Elisha had grown deeper in his own relationship with the Lord and was ready to act on his own. It wasn't sufficient that he merely be chosen by God to take Elijah's place; the ultimate goal was that he actually lived it. The goal of this sonship process, as evidenced by the Elisha Way, is for the son to receive the mantle and step into his own spiritual calling. While some element of separation anxiety may exist, discipleship cannot be successful without the release of the individual into his own destiny.

It is important to note that this separation does not apply to the love and affection expressed by our fathers for the Word of God is clear that nothing can ever separate us from the love of Christ.

> *Who shall separate us from the love of Christ? Shall tribulation, or distress, or persecution, or famine, or nakedness, or peril, or sword?*
> -Romans 8:35-36, NKJV

Just as it is an act of love for a father to release his son to become a man, it is also an act of love and the evidence of the love that God has for us, for a spiritual father to release his spiritual son into his own place of ministry. This release is not a loss, but rather an extension of the father's own success through the success of the son. To adapt an old saying, it can be rightly said that a spiritual father has not succeeded until those who are his spiritual children have succeeded.

Father/Son Imagery in Scripture

We cannot go wrong by applying father/son imagery to this process of discipleship. It is not only apparent in the life of Elijah and Elisha, and in the lives of Jesus and His disciples, but its imagery is common throughout the New Testament. In fact, Paul calls both Titus and Timothy "true sons" (1 Timothy 1:2; Titus 1:4).

True discipleship has not changed since Jesus used it to train those who would carry His message. Jesus summarized the nature of discipleship when He described his own life and actions in the book of John.

Then Jesus answered and said to them, "Most assuredly, I say to you, the Son can do nothing of Himself, but what He sees the Father do; for whatever He does, the Son also does in like manner. For the Father loves the Son, and shows Him all things that He Himself does; and He will show Him greater works than these, that you may marvel.

-John 5:19-21, NKJV

While we must be careful to not take this passage out of context, it clearly indicates that in His own father/son relationship, Jesus held the example

31

of the Father in the highest of esteem. If true discipleship relationships are to flourish again within the Christian community, we must first remember that the example of the Father in Heaven must be held in the highest regard. Then and only then, can we follow those who follow Him.

While we have often considered the passage in Luke regarding the return of Elijah, in this context of discipleship, it seems to take on new meaning. The words penned by Luke in his gospel were not original, but in fact a recitation of prophecy in Malachi 4:5-6 regarding the coming Messiah.

> *He will also go before Him in the spirit and power of Elijah, 'to turn the hearts of the fathers to the children,' and the disobedient to the wisdom of the just, to make ready a people prepared for the Lord."*
> -Luke 1:17, NKJV

I believe that, just as it was foretold that Elijah must precede the first coming of Jesus, it is likely that he must precede the second coming of the Jesus. Certainly, his role is the same: to return the hearts of the fathers to the children. As we draw ever closer to the return of Christ, it is essential that we heed the call of Elijah and begin to prepare the way for the return of our Lord. By taking up the Elisha Way of discipleship, we will see the hearts of the spiritual fathers turned once again to the children, and perhaps the old adage – like father, like son – will prove true.

In so doing, we will witness the cycle of fathers training sons who go on to become fathers who train their sons.

Chapter 3
BECOMING A SPIRITUAL FATHER

Becoming a spiritual father is a challenge greater than most of us have ever imagined. We have buried our head in the sand and delegated the responsibilities of fatherhood to pastors. In this process of delegation, the church has become satisfied to sit back and let someone else do the work of the ministry for them. Ephesians 4 designates apostles, prophets, evangelists, pastors, and teachers to equip the saints to do the work of the ministry. It is important to note that true spiritual fathers will not come solely from those we identify with the five-fold ministry of Ephesians 4, but rather from among all of the saints.

Our Commission to be Spiritual Fathers

In examining the story of Elijah and Elisha, much can be learned about what it takes to become a spiritual father, as well as what it takes to become a spiritual son. It seems that today's potential Elisha generation will not be satisfied with hearing about the miracles of old, but rather a generation of believers who want to see it for themselves. It would also seem that this kind of desire for personal experience was not lost on Elisha either.

> He also took up the mantle of Elijah that had fallen from him, and went back and stood by the bank of the Jordan. Then he took the mantle of Elijah that had fallen from him, and struck the water, and said, "Where is the LORD God of Elijah?" And when he also had struck the water, it was divided this way and that; and Elisha crossed over.
>
> -2 Kings 2:13-14, NKJV

Elisha was clearly looking for evidence that he had received the double portion of the spirit of Elijah when he cried out, "Where is the Lord God of Elijah?" This was not the call of a man who lacked confidence in his God, but rather it was a challenge issued for all the spiritual world to hear. The cry that came forth from the mouth of this spiritual son was almost indignant. There was a clear recognition that circumstances were changing and that if Elijah's God did not become the God of Elisha, then there was no need to continue.

"Where is the LORD God of Elijah" was a call for the God of Elisha's spiritual father to show up and be real for a maturing spiritual son. Elisha would no longer serve the God of his father, but rather the God of his father must now become his own. This is the

36

God that we need today – a God who is real and living and interacts with his creation to touch and transform, but also to flow through the lives of those who would be His sons.

It seems that a cry echoes throughout the church today among the young men and women who are looking for real authority. It is, however, with great sorrow that we must recognize that their cry is different. The present-day generation has been all but abandoned by the church, and spiritual fathers have been so scarce that the cry sounds more like, "Where are the Elijahs of the Lord God?"

It would appear that a strong demonic attack has swept through the church and gone almost unnoticed. This assault on the church intended to destroy this present Elisha generation by leaving them fatherless and depositing an orphan spirit among them. There is only one way to defeat this attack: the Elijahs of God must arise and begin pouring out their lives into the generation that will follow them. If we are truly living in a Kingdom age, then it is essential for this restoration to occur. Perhaps it is even a necessary fulfillment of prophecy in order for the Lord's return to be ushered into place. We cannot expect a generation of orphans to become the bride without spot or wrinkle or blemish that Jesus is expecting (Ephesians 5:27).

We must assume that we have been living in a Kingdom age (at least since the time of Christ). John the Baptist, the forerunner of Jesus, proclaimed this very message.

> *In those days John the Baptist came preaching in the wilderness of Judea, and saying, "Repent, for the kingdom of heaven is at hand!" For this is he who was spoken of by the prophet Isaiah, saying: "The voice of one crying in the wilderness: 'Prepare the way of the LORD; Make His paths straight.'"*
>
> -Matthew 3:1-2, NKJV

John's proclamation that the Kingdom was at hand was accompanied by his recitation of Isaiah's prophecy that he was to "prepare the way of the Lord" (Isaiah 40:3). Jesus told His disciples to go, preach, that the kingdom of heaven is at hand (Matthew 10:7). As a result, we can assume that we have the same job given to John the Baptist– we are to prepare the way of the Lord. The Great Commission itself indicates that we have been sent to all the world.

> *And Jesus came and spoke to them, saying, "All authority has been given to Me in heaven and on earth. Go therefore and make disciples of all the nations, baptizing them in the name of the Father and of the Son and of the Holy Spirit, teaching them to observe all things that I have commanded you; and lo, I am with you always, even to the end of the age." Amen.*
>
> -Matthew 28:18-20, NKJV

38

We have been woefully lacking in the establishment of the fathers who are necessary to raise up these disciples.

What has hindered us from accomplishing our calling? The orphan spirit has violently attacked the foundation of relationships and severely weakened our ability to impart spiritual wisdom from generation to generation. This violent assault by the enemy has been met with little more than passive resistance. If true spiritual fathers are to arrive on the scene, then this passive resistance must end and we must acknowledge the words that Jesus spoke when He said:

> *And from the days of John the Baptist until now the kingdom of heaven suffers violence, and the violent take it by force.*
> -Matthew 11:12-13, NKJV

Notice how John's proclamation of the coming kingdom and Jesus' description of the kingdom's present-day reality go hand in hand. The kingdom is at hand, but it has suffered violence since the day it was proclaimed. The violent world of the enemy has been usurping the kingdom since its inception. Now it's time for spiritual fathers to fight for the right of their spiritual children to inherit the kingdom.

So then, if we are to fulfill our present day commission, then we too must take up the mantle of Elijah and first begin to turn the hearts of the fathers to the children and then continue to see the hearts of

Pastor Roberts message that Gifts that you have don't matter because God has created you to do that.

the children turned to their fathers. Spiritual fathers must arise from the everyday ranks of the Church and a faceless generation must be equipped to fulfill their destiny. In the pursuit of this destiny, we must remember that the children are certainly entitled to a double portion, but the fathers must have a portion to double. Zero multiplied by zero equals zero. If spiritual fathers have nothing to give, then there can never be a generation that walks in the double portion anointing.

The Elijah Task is Challenging

The task given to the Elijah generation cannot be taken lightly, for it is far more challenging in many respects than that which has been given to the Elisha generation. After all, if the Elisha generation is to emerge, it cannot occur until the Elijahs blaze a path before them. The Elisha generation needs to use the ceiling of the Elijah generation's anointing as the floor for their own building process.

What does the process of becoming a spiritual father look like? For starters, it requires the Elijah generation be willing to endure the adversity that brings maturity. The book of James provides additional insight into true maturity.

You know that under pressure, your faith-life is forced into the open and shows its true colors. So don't try to get out of

Relationship

Many Have Church Relegated to a Place ⇒ Not a Person

anything prematurely. Let it do its work so you become mature and well-developed, not deficient in any way.
-James 1:3-4, The Message

It is the pressures and trials of life that bring us to the place of maturity. Without them, we will never grow or become be a true Elijah generation. Elijah himself arrived on the scene in one of Israel's darkest hours, and that darkness at times seemed to overwhelm him. Yet, in its midst he endured, persevered, and overcame. He walked with authority and in an anointing that caused others to be drawn to him, but it also caused the violent forces of darkness to seek to overthrow him. Out of these trials emerged a man with something to give. Out of these adversities came someone with a portion that could be doubled.

A subtle deception has sought to filter through the church for generations. The enemy attempts to convince the church that a Christian life is an easy life. Even within the teachings of the church itself, we have seen a generation raised with the idea that we should not be facing challenges, and that our faith should be sufficient to result in a life of plenty. This dangerous faith teaching has damaged the integrity of those who would be spiritual fathers by instilling a false sense of security and an aversion to adversity. Adversity is the birthplace of greatness and it cannot, nor should it be avoided. The Word of God instructs us to become over-comers. We must overcome obstacles for this status to come into existence in our lives.

It has been said that great battles produce great warriors and result in great victories, while small battles produce small warriors and result in small victories. The spiritual fathers of this generation can afford to be nothing less than great warriors. As a result, they must expect to fight great battles and see great victories. This principle is clearly present in the life of Elijah himself.

The first mention of Elijah in scripture is found deep in the context of adversity. 1 Kings 16 proclaims that Israel is being ruled by the evil Ahab. It is said that Ahab did more to provoke the Lord God to anger than all the kings of Israel who went before him (1 Kings 16:33). Ahab is married to Jezebel, whose very name has become synonymous with the concept of subtle manipulation and control. Elijah is thrust upon the scene in the midst of a generation fixed upon evil and immorality. He arrives with a powerful message that such wickedness will not be tolerated in the land and a proclamation of drought that will produce a powerful demonstration of God's authority. These conditions conflict with the false world of ease so often proclaimed by the modern day message of hyper-faith.

In order to become a true spiritual father, Elijah was forced to mature. Not only did the wicked suffer the effects of a more than three-year drought, but Elijah faced the same challenges. During this season, Elijah learned to expect the provision of the Lord – it was the only way he survived. By the time Elijah finally heard the voice of the Lord directing him to present himself to Ahab, to confront the prophets of Baal, and to proclaim an end to the drought, he had reached a point where he saw himself as abandoned and alone. In the face of this adversity (which was a greater challenge than the lack of water itself), Elijah was called to demonstrate the power of God, and do so while facing 400 prophets of Baal.

God demonstrated his authority and the prophets of Baal were defeated, yet almost immediately Elijah faced another obstacle. Suddenly, on the heels of so great a victory, Elijah was fleeing for his life, hiding in a cave, and struggling with the issues of depression, fear, anxiety, and self-pity. Elijah dealt with not only the physical hardships brought about by the days of drought, but also with spiritual, mental, and emotional hardships brought on by his conflict with Jezebel. It is only after these challenges were conquered that the real authority of spiritual fathering appeared on the scene.

Growth comes in the midst of adversity; however, we tend to see its evidence only when things are going well, and thereby attribute the growth itself to those seasons of peace. We often fail to recognize that the fruit we see in the times of peace is a result of the seeds sown during the times of trial. Notice the commission that God gave Elijah.

Then the LORD said to him: "Go, return on your way to the Wilderness of Damascus; and when you arrive, anoint Hazael as king over Syria. Also you shall anoint Jehu the son of Nimshi as king over Israel. And Elisha the son of Shaphat of Abel Meholah you shall anoint as prophet in your place. It shall be that whoever escapes the sword of Hazael, Jehu will kill; and whoever escapes the sword of Jehu, Elisha will kill. Yet I have reserved seven thousand in Israel, all whose knees have not bowed to Baal, and every mouth that has not kissed him."

-1 Kings 19:15-18, NKJV

God commissioned Elijah to raise up warriors to stand with him and face the evil of his day. Hazael, Jehu, and Elisha could not have received their call until Elijah had faced the fires of testing that developed him into a true spiritual father. Elisha's call as a spiritual son, one to take Elijah's place as prophet, could only come after Elijah had overcome the adversity that the Lord allowed to be set before him. Such adversity arose in Elijah's life in order to allow him to obtain something he could pass on.

With such an example as this, it is difficult to see how anyone could expect to become a true spiritual father while living a life of comfort and ease. Warriors are not drawn to the places of peace, but rather to the places of war. The kingdom of heaven must be forcibly taken, and adversity is a necessary part of that process. We must always remember that while God does not remove adversity from the lives of those destined to become spiritual fathers, he does provide all that is needed to overcome and to obtain the great victories. As we learn what it takes to become a true spiritual father, we quickly understand that it's a considerable undertaking.

Chapter 4
BECOMING A SPIRITUAL SON

Like spiritual fathers, the sons have responsibilities too. Becoming a true spiritual son is not something that we can simply decide to do one day. It's not something to be taken lightly. Just as in real life, the child has no influence over who their parents will be.

The modern-day conference scene is filled with examples of individuals who are desperately seeking to be adopted. These groupies spend lots of time visiting churches in an effort to be noticed by those who they esteem in the spiritual world. While I certainly do not intend to criticize their hunger for knowledge and spiritual understanding, the idea that they will be great because they have shadowed someone they consider great is far removed from the spiritual growth resulting from the parent/child relationship. Those who seek only to follow in order to gain an occasional benefit or blessing will rarely glean any true knowledge or spiritual understanding.

Simply put, disciples are called by the one who will disciple them. In other words, we don't get to pick our mentor, but rather they pick us. This may be a literal, spoken call as with Jesus and his disciples, or it may be a symbolic gesture as when Elijah threw his mantle over Elisha. Whether spoken or symbolic, one thing is clear: spiritual fathers are charged with the onus of choosing a spiritual son and not the other way around. It is from this type of selection process that a true spiritual strength will emerge.

The Conscription Process

Conscription is an act of recruitment for a purpose. Examples of conscription can help us to understand the importance of the process by which spiritual sons should be chosen.

When a nation's military finds itself in need of recruits, it doesn't wait for individuals to recognize the need and come to the aid of their nation. Rather, conscription has been the historic method of obtaining new soldiers. In America, the Selective Service is the entity responsible for conscription. The name itself implies that discernment is used in determining who can actually fulfill the necessary obligations. A set of criteria exist against which every individual is measured. Some will fail at the most basic level, as they have not yet reached the proper physical age or maturity level. Still others will pass these minimum requirements, but fail when it comes to other standards, such as those who are flatfooted or have vision problems. Even after passing these physical requirements, still others will fail during the pressures of basic training. Of those who endure thus far, a selected few may advance to Officers Candidate School (where a whole new set of selection criteria awaits them).

In the spiritual arena, this example reminds us of the warfare to which we are called. God has established His own set of selection criteria and He is the one who recruits us. He takes us through a process of preparation until the day that He determines that we are ready to enter into the battlefield as fully trained soldiers. Some will be chosen to enter the battle as foot soldiers and others as generals. One is not better than the other, but each have separate skills and expertise that allow them to fulfill the role for which they have been selected.

The second example comes from the world of sports. In this arena, a process also known as the draft is used to select the top athletes. Every high school and college athlete has dreamed of playing for their sport's version of the NFL or NBA. Today, many such dreams actually begin in little league sports. After years of waiting and preparation, of try-outs and practices, of game day victories and defeats, the day of the draft finally arrives. It is a lifetime of effort and achievement that prepares one for this day; yet when it arrives, it is totally out of the control of that individual. They may have worked for countless hours to make themselves the best in the world, yet someone else will decide the number one draft pick. Some will be devastated that they did not make the top ten, while others will feel fortunate to have been picked at all.

Though many young men and women may dread the military version of the draft, in the world of sports, this day is a day of excitement and celebration. Whereas the military draft chooses men and women who will fill the front lines, the sports draft chooses the best of the best to become champions in their field and role models for a generation. In the spiritual sense, this draft reminds us that spiritual sons are called to be champions of the faith and ultimately spiritual fathers, role models for the next generation. While God does not determine who is number one among those He chooses (all are of equal value in His eyes). It is to some degree within our own control what we become after we're chosen.

Matthew 22:14 states that many are called, but few are chosen. In the context of spiritual fathering, this scripture reminds us that we have all been called to become the sons of God (Galatians 3:26), to receive the free gift of eternal life. However, it also reminds us that not all who have been called to this place of salvation are chosen as spiritual sons to ultimately be set into places of authority as spiritual fathers themselves. This elevated state of sonship is described in the book of Revelation.

> *And He said to me, "It is done! I am the Alpha and the Omega, the Beginning and the End. I will give of the fountain of the*

50

*water of life freely to him who thirsts. He
who overcomes shall inherit all things, and
I will be his God and he shall be My son.*
                                    -Rev 21:6-7, NKJV

Our Heavenly Father will give the living water of
life freely to him who thirsts, and thus salvation is
assured. However, we find that the bar is higher for
sonship. In order to recognize our true potential, to be
spiritual sons who beget other spiritual sons, we must
not merely just get by, but rather we must overcome.

Before focusing on the qualifications of a true
spiritual son, it is important to further delineate the
selection process from a Biblical perspective using
three specific examples:

- Selection of the disciples by Jesus
- Selection of John Mark by Barnabas
- Selection of Elisha by Elijah

Jesus and His Disciples – The Call is Personal

While the terminology may be difficult to grasp,
the Scriptures identify the ultimate spiritual father as
the one whom we identify as the Son. Jesus is the
ultimate role model of all things spiritual, including
the proper process of being a father in the spiritual
realm. By examining His selection method, we can
learn valuable lessons about how this process works.

Jesus related to the disciples on the level where
He found them. He met them where they were. Peter

51

and Andrew were rough and rugged fishermen and when Jesus encountered them, He did so in language that they could understand. Matthew recounts their initial meeting.

> *And Jesus, walking by the Sea of Galilee, saw two brothers, Simon called Peter, and Andrew his brother, casting a net into the sea; for they were fishermen. Then He said to them, "Follow Me, and I will make you fishers of men." They immediately left their nets and followed Him.*
> -Matt 4:18-20, NKJV

He called Peter and Andrew to become fishers of men, not carpenters for Christ. Jesus himself had been a carpenter and the idea of building the kingdom would have been part of His own life experiences, but to these fishermen, it would have been totally foreign. Jesus' actions demonstrate that a call to sonship should be relevant and personal.

Jesus changed His method of invitation based upon the individuals to whom He was speaking. When he came upon Levi, the tax collector, He approached him in a manner that he would understand. Jesus didn't speak to this tax collector in the same way that He had called the fishermen. Instead, He simply said, "Follow me" (Mark 2:14). This approach was much more of a command than an invitation (something Levi was accustomed to hearing as he worked for the Roman government). As He did with the other disciples, Jesus met Levi where he was.

To become a true spiritual son, we must be open and ready to receive that personal call of a spiritual father. We may have our own ideas about how things should transpire; however, God meets us in a personal way and extends His invitation to us on a personal level. If we are called to be an altar worker, God will not send an Apostle to be our spiritual father. On the other hand, if we are called to be a prophetic voice, then God will not send one gifted for hospital visitation. While our calling may change as we grow over time, our spiritual fathers will impart what we need for that season. God will send exactly whom you need, and will make the invitation a personal one.

Barnabas & John Mark – The Call Will Meet You Where You Are

John Mark provides an interesting profile of a spiritual son. The book of Acts indicates that together Barnabas and Paul (Saul) chose John Mark to travel with them and become a spiritual son to them.

> *And Barnabas and Saul returned from Jerusalem when they had fulfilled their ministry, and they also took with them John whose surname was Mark.*
> -Acts 12:25, NKJV

While this seemed to be an exciting beginning with tremendous potential, something happened along the way that threatened to jeopardize the entire process. By the end of Acts chapter 15, a serious threat to John Mark's sonship developed and there was a real question as to whether the father/son relationship would continue to exist.

> *Then after some days Paul said to Barnabas, "Let us now go back and visit our brethren in every city where we have preached the word of the Lord, and see how they are doing." Now Barnabas was determined to take with them John called Mark. But Paul insisted that they should not take with them the one who had departed from them in Pamphylia, and had not gone with them to the work. Then the contention became so sharp that they parted from one another. And so Barnabas took Mark and sailed to Cyprus; but Paul chose Silas and departed, being commended by the brethren to the grace of God. And he went through Syria and Cilicia, strengthening the churches.*
>
> -Acts 15:36-41, NKJV

We don't know exactly what happened among Barnabas, Paul, and John Mark during their journey, but it must have been something significant. All we know for sure is whatever transpired did result in John Mark's departure and return home without fulfilling his commitments to the mission. This conflict created a break in the relationship between Paul and John Mark. In fact, the breach was so serious that it carried through the relationship between Paul and Barnabas.

One may consider how this story relates to becoming a spiritual son, because on the surface, it appears to have more to do with destruction of relationships rather than establishment of them. However, when we dig a little deeper, it becomes apparent that something more has happened.

Barnabas always serves as a champion of the underdog's cause. His very name means "son of encouragement" and he lived up to that name on more than one occasion. Actually, it is questionable whether Paul would have ever reached this point in his ministry had not been for Barnabas. Here we find Barnabas effectively releasing Paul to his own destiny and choosing to champion a difficult cause. So great is Barnabas' love for John Mark that he actually risks his relationship with Paul (who is clearly now capable of standing on his own two feet) in order to ensure that John Mark (who appears to be barely able to crawl) is given another chance.

The lesson learned from this exchange is vital to the understanding of what it takes to become a true spiritual son. This passage opens our eyes to the understanding that it is God who chooses for us, not we who choose for Him. God had chosen John Mark for a special task, and He intended for John Mark's good work to come to completion. The spiritual father that God had prepared for John Mark was unwilling to see him fail. He was willing to extend the call and meet Mark where Mark was to insure that he would one day succeed.

Perhaps John Mark, in a desperation to be like Paul, had manipulated the circumstances to ensure his inclusion in that first mission trip. (Maybe he would have been considered a modern day groupie of the Apostle Paul.) We do not have the answers to these questions, but is whether John Mark had pursued Paul or Paul had pursued him, the spiritual son ship was not Paul's to grant. It was in the hands of Barnabas.

This story should give us hope. While it may not be our job to choose our spiritual father, we can rest assured that God will orchestrate our lives to such a degree that our spiritual father will find us. Furthermore, there is no substitute for the impartation that comes from the one whom God has ordained.

If this were the end of John Mark's story, it would have been sufficient, but there is still more. After many years, the value of forging such a strong father/son relationship becomes apparent not only to John Mark, but to the church of his day and to believers throughout history. Later in life, during one of his terms of imprisonment Paul wrote the following words to Timothy.

> *Only Luke is with me. Get Mark and bring him with you, for he is useful to me for ministry.*
> -2 Timothy 4:11-12, NKJV

These words give us final confirmation of the value that becoming a true spiritual son can have in our lives, as here Paul requested the very same man whom he once rejected so firmly that he parted ways with Barnabas. The rational for requesting John Mark is of equal significance to the request itself, as Paul now considers this young man useful to him for ministry. This illustration reminds us that when we are willing to pay the price and glean from the life of the one that God has ordained to father us, then we ultimately become more valuable to the Kingdom, even though that value might take time to recognize. No longer was John Mark merely a spiritual son to Barnabas, but he had become known by all as one useful for the advancement of the kingdom. The call that met him where he was, had now taken him on a journey of hardship, rejection, and perhaps even ridicule, and had ultimately delivered him to a place beyond his expectations.

Elijah and Elisha – The Call is for the Son to Accept

As we have seen, the relationship between Elijah and Elisha is filled with lessons on the father/son relationship. On this topic, the initial interaction between the two provides us a final piece of valuable insight into the way the process works.

So he departed from there, and found Elisha the son of Shaphat, who was plowing with twelve yoke of oxen before

him, and he was with the twelfth. Then
Elijah passed by him and threw his mantle
on him. And he left the oxen and ran after
Elijah, and said, "Please let me kiss my
father and my mother, and then I will
follow you. "And he said to him, "Go back
again, for what have I done to you?"

-1 Kings 19:19-20, NKJV

Certainly, no words inviting Elisha to become a spiritual son were actually spoken. Instead, God used imagery to convey His message. By throwing his mantle upon Elisha, Elijah indicated that he would provide a spiritual covering for the chosen Elisha.

However, it must also be remembered that this challenge issued by Elijah was more than a mere symbolic gesture. It was an invitation that must first be accepted by Elisha; it could not be forced upon him. Elijah's statement "what have I done to thee" indicates that he did not wish to place any constraint upon Elisha, but rather gave him liberty to choose to follow a call issued by God as opposed to one issued by Elijah. Some may assume that Elijah is chiding Elisha for his desire to go and bid his parents farewell, but this is not the case. In a more modern context, Elijah's statement could be interpreted as, "I haven't offered you anything Elisha, it was God who offered. If you need to go and kiss your father and mother and God has told you it was alright, then it is fine with me, make up your mind and let's get on with the Father's business."

This example offers us a tremendous challenge. Because God will not force us to accept His invitation to become a spiritual son, there is potential for us to carry a tremendous burden if we do not heed His voice. The acceptance of the invitation is ours alone to give; however, failure to hear the call of God has its own set of consequences, not the least of which is that His voice becomes harder to hear in the future. We should also recognize that the call to this father/son discipleship has not come through an audible voice of God in any of our examples (remembering that Jesus operated in the earth as fully man). Each invitation came at the hands of human flesh by way of the one who would be the father figure, and thus, we can reasonably expect that our own invitation will come in much the same way. This requires discernment on our part, so that we may learn to hear the Heavenly Father's voice, as He speaks through the mouth and actions of His servants. Perhaps this is the first step to becoming a spiritual son.

The Neighborhood Kids

True spiritual fathers do not ignore the other children in the community, but rather choose to pour out a special impartation into the lives of the ones that God has instructed them to lead. Clearly, there were multitudes that followed after Jesus to learn from his teaching. Jesus did not turn them away; yet, His deepest insight was reserved for those quiet times with His disciples. Additionally, while Elisha was Elijah's spiritual son, we know from 2 Kings Chapter 2 and various other passages, that Elijah certainly had relationships with other individuals as well. In fact, it would appear that these other individuals felt as though their relationship with Elijah was equal to or even exceeded the relationship that Elisha enjoyed. Notice how they spoke to Elisha, as the time approached for Elijah to ascend into heaven.

> *Now the sons of the prophets who were at Bethel came out to Elisha, and said to him, "Do you know that the LORD will take away your master from over you today?" And he said, "Yes, I know; keep silent!"*
> -2 Kings 2:3, NKJV

This same pattern repeated in each town that Elijah and Elisha visited. While this pattern suggests that these sons of the prophets were hearing the plans of God, it also suggests something further. It would appear that these men felt that their relationship with God (and perhaps even with Elijah) was sufficiently greater than Elisha's, and knew something about Elijah that Elisha himself didn't know.

We know of the role that Elijah played in establishing schools of the prophets. We can assume that he may have even known some of the men longer than he had known Elisha. Perhaps Elijah had even spent individual time with men in these schools and instructed them in the things of the Lord. Whatever the relationship that these men perceived that they had, it was not evil in any way. Neither Elijah nor Elisha gave any indication that the men were presumptuous. A relationship clearly existed, albeit, not on the same level as the relationship with Elisha. Basically, these men were like the neighborhood kids – children whom Elijah loved and poured a part of his life into – but they were not his true spiritual sons.

Notice the response that Elisha gave the men, "Yes, I know; keep silent!" This response alone shows us that Elisha's relationship was of a more significant character. He had the authority to silence these men, and received no negative reaction to this stern acknowledgement and rebuke. Additionally, we can see the difference in the relationships by what transpires later. It was Elisha (not the sons of the prophets) who traveled with Elijah and saw him ascend into heaven. When Elisha returned it was apparent that he had an impartation of much greater significance than any of them had enjoyed, for the spirit of Elijah rested on Elisha.

Chapter 5

QUALIFICATIONS OF A SPIRITUAL SON

Although a spiritual son does not choose his spiritual father, it is the responsibility of such an individual to be prepared to be chosen. The first problem faced by those who would be true spiritual sons is to overcome the desire to make it happen themselves. The second problem faced by those who would be true spiritual sons is the temptation to sit back and wait for it to happen. There are two kinds of waiting – active and passive. When individuals recognize that they must wait to be chosen, it becomes easy to slip into the pattern of passive waiting; however, this will ultimately delay the process. In order to hasten the selection, a true spiritual son must learn to engage in active waiting.

Active Waiting

Active waiting is the concept whereby a person is learning the virtues associated with James' explanation of real patience.

> *My brethren, count it all joy when you fall*
> *into various trials, knowing that the testing*
> *of your faith produces patience. But let*
> *patience have its perfect work, that you*
> *may be perfect and complete, lacking*
> *nothing.*
>
> -James 1:2-4, NKJV

This passage seems to indicate that there is more to waiting than just sitting around and twiddling your thumbs. James explains that patience is best produced out of the fiery furnace of tests and trials. Generally as we face the problems in life, we don't learn to just sit back and take it, but instead we learn how to respond in order to overcome. If our objective is to completely fulfill our destiny, then we need this type of patience. In learning this patience and taking this journey, we also move closer to our goal of true spiritual sonship.

Waiting should be a season of preparation that prepares us for the next move of God in our lives. The Godly character built within us while actively waiting upon the Lord strengthens us and prepares us to press in without growing weary (Isaiah 40:31; 2 Thessalonians 3:13). After Elijah gave King Ahab the prophetic word that it wouldn't rain until he said so, even this prophetic father learned to actively wait (1 Kings 17). When this prophetic utterance was spoken, Elijah had no idea how long it would be before God would once again send rain upon the land. He had to wait, just like everyone else. While it would have been easier for Elijah to use his open line of communication with God and be among the first to know that it was time for the rain to return, we must remember that God did not tell him. When we examine what Elijah did during this time of waiting, we find that he was very active. Actually, Elijah endured many difficult trials between the proclamation of drought and the return of rain.

How many times do we ask God when He is going to use us? Have we ever asked ourselves whether we're active while we wait? God may very well have called you to be an Apostle to the Nations, but until the fulfillment of that word, what will you have been doing? Are you sitting back and waiting for the world to recognize you or, like Elijah, are you diligently pursuing the tasks at hand? We shouldn't value our call so highly that we can't see the opportunities for service that exist around us while we wait for that call to be fulfilled. If we take the first steps in our preparation as spiritual son and we can use the time of waiting to build Godly character and establish the qualities in our lives that ensure our eligibility for selection. If we are unwilling to do this ourselves, it seems clear from scripture that God will nudge us in this direction anyway. Though the comfort of doing nothing may be what we want, we will never be able to obtain it. The Psalmist makes this clear.

Until the time his word came to pass, The Word of the Lord tested him.

-Psalm 105:19, NKJV

Cultivating a Work Ethic

It appears clear that Godly patience, expressed through active waiting, is essential to our journey toward spiritual sonship. What then are the characteristics that we are seeking to develop during such a period of time? We certainly don't have sufficient room in the pages of this book to examine all of the qualities that God desires to instill within us in order to prepare us for His selection, however, Elisha's life does identify some that can be highlighted. Everything that we know about the life of Elisha prior to being called by Elijah is summed up in three verses.

> *So he departed from there, and found Elisha the son of Shaphat, who was plowing with twelve yoke of oxen before him, and he was with the twelfth. Then Elijah passed by him and threw his mantle on him. And he left the oxen and ran after Elijah, and said, "Please let me kiss my father and my mother, and then I will follow you."*
> *And he said to him, "Go back again, for what have I done to you?"*
> *So Elisha turned back from him, and took a yoke of oxen and slaughtered them and*

boiled their flesh, using the oxen's equipment, and gave it to the people, and they ate. Then he arose and followed Elijah, and became his servant.

-1 Kings 19:19-21, NKJV

While this may seem like very little, we can glean a number of things from this passage as to what qualities Elisha had been honing prior to his selection by Elijah. As we examine Elisha's life before the mantle was tossed upon him, it may help us to better understand why he was so successful afterward. First, we find Elisha hard at work in the field. It is possible that Elisha had been crying out to the Lord and seeking for some indication of his gifts and calls. Maybe he had been praying and asking God to show him what he could do to contribute to the kingdom. Certainly his heart was turned to the Lord, for only days earlier the Lord had directly spoken to Elijah and told him that it would be Elisha who would follow in his footsteps (1 Kings 19:16). What we know from verses 19-21 is that he was diligently working when his soon-to-be father arrived.

It is significant to note that Elijah didn't find Elisha in the synagogue, focused on the rituals of prayer and study. Though we might expect this out of those destined to become the voice of the Lord to Israel, it was not the case for Elisha. He was not busy with religious things, but rather he was about his (earthly) father's business. Oftentimes, people want to be religious rather than industrious. Although no religious practices are described in the narrative of Elisha's call their absence is not an indication that he was unprepared. On the other hand, the references to his hard working attitude and actions seem to indicate that such qualities were desired by the Lord.

Consider Elisha's actions in comparison to the parable presented by Jesus.

> *"A faithful, sensible servant is one to whom the master can give the responsibility of managing his other household servants and feeding them. If the master returns and finds that the servant has done a good job, there will be a reward. I tell you the truth, the master will put that servant in charge of all he owns.*
> -Matthew 24:45-47, NLT

Elisha was a man who was serving the Lord where he was. He was busy managing the household and feeding the family. While there can be no question that his heart was turned to the Lord, it is also clear that he was faithful in the day-to-day affairs of life. Elisha was faithfully serving in the little things, yet having no idea that he would one day be set over much greater things. When Elijah arrived, he found Elisha busy and working. This was exactly what God was looking for.

Grumbling and complaining over the tasks at hand will not advance the Kingdom of Heaven. Elisha was not afraid to work in the field, and it would appear that his attitude was right as well. When the Lord spoke to Elijah about Elisha, He speaks of "Elisha the son of Shaphat of Abel Meholah" (1 Kings 19:16). It is interesting to note that Abel Meholah (the place of Elisha's family) means "meadow of dancing"[9], thus indicating that the work of Elisha's hands as he labored in the field was a joy and not a burden.

Clearing Away Hindrances

While Elisha was working diligently when Elijah approached him, he was also ready, willing, and able to respond. Elijah's throwing of his mantle across Elisha's shoulders is of great significance, and Elisha wastes absolutely no time in responding. Elisha's immediate reply is to leave the oxen behind and run to follow after Elijah. This passage implies that Elijah didn't even stop as he passed by (perhaps in much the same way that Jesus passed by the disciples on the Sea of Galilee). It was essential that Elisha be ready to respond, or the opportunity would certainly have passed him by. Obviously, Elisha had learned the lesson that the writer of Hebrews would set for hundreds of years later.

Therefore we also, since we are surrounded by so great a cloud of

---

[9] The Online Bible Thayer's Greek Lexicon and Brown Driver & Briggs Hebrew Lexicon, Copyright (c)1993, Woodside Bible Fellowship, Ontario, Canada.

> *witnesses, let us lay aside every weight,*
> *and the sin which so easily ensnares us,*
> *and let us run with endurance the race that*
> *is set before us,*
>
> -Hebrews 12:1, NKJV

Elisha laid aside everything that hindered him (including the very oxen that had only moments before been his greatest asset) to pursue his calling. The farm work could easily have ensnared Elisha had he attempted to stick to the job that was before him, instead of recognizing the call.

We must recognize that it is often tempting to grow comfortable in the work that we are currently doing and miss the calling of God to change and move on. Elisha seems to have known that even good things could be a hindrance if they are elevated above the directives of the Lord. If we are going to adopt Elisha's strong work ethic, then we must also adopt his ability to discern between that which is good and that which is God. Working in the field was a good thing, and until only moments before it had been a God thing, but in the twinkle of an eye, all had changed and God was on the move. Elisha was aware that in response to the call of God, delay is as sinful as refusal. Of course, we would never tell the Lord *"no"* when he calls, but have we learned the lesson from Elisha in that we won't tell him *"wait"*?

Cherishing Loyalty

Some would argue that Elisha was not as quick to answer the call of God as was suggested in the preceding section. The basis for this argument is Elisha's first verbal response requesting time to see his family instead of immediately accepting the call. To read this passage in such a way is to misunderstand the loyalty that Elisha had to his family and to his community. Elisha was not asking to delay his obedience, but rather for the opportunity to show honor to whom honor was due.

Elisha had been trained by his father and mother in the way he should go (Proverbs 22:6). He could not forget his loyalty to those who had helped him reach this point in his life. By acting in such a way, he honored those who had poured into his life.

In today's society, we have all but lost the sense of honor and loyalty that Elisha recognized. Years ago, people would work as many as 40 years for the same company. In contrast, today the average worker moves to a new job every two or three years. Likewise, many Christians flit from one spiritual leader to another and fail to recognize the value of what has been instilled within us by the effort of those leaders. All of those who have been leaders to us may not have been destined to be spiritual fathers; nevertheless, the time and energy they pour out of themselves helped to prepare us for sonship selection. We need to show honor and loyalty to the leaders in our lives.

Choosing to Sacrifice

We cannot overlook Elisha's sacrificial offering. Elisha slaughtered his oxen, used the yoke and other equipment from the field to build the fire for cooking the meat, and fed his family and friends before he left with Elijah. This was a sacrifice of significant proportion. Elijah understood that the call of God comes with a price, and he was already prepared to pay that price before Elijah passed him by.

While there can be no doubt that the actual physical cost of Elisha's sacrifice of these oxen and his equipment was significant, there were other symbolic implications. Elisha's sacrifice was also an irrevocable commitment to his journey. By surrendering the items of his financial livelihood, Elisha expressed that nothing would draw him away from this call of God. He would leave no opportunity for the enemy to lure him with the things of his old life.

Elisha made two sacrifices that day: the oxen and his own life. He presented himself to the Lord and proclaimed that he would not look back. He understood this same idea that Jesus spoke of.

> But Jesus said to him, "No one, having put his hand to the plow, and looking back, is fit for the kingdom of God."
> -Luke 9:62, NKJV

Elisha made himself a living sacrifice to the Lord as described in Romans.

I beseech you therefore, brethren, by the mercies of God, that you present your bodies a living sacrifice, holy, acceptable to God, which is your reasonable service. And do not be conformed to this world, but be transformed by the renewing of your mind, that you may prove what is that good and acceptable and perfect will of God.
-Romans 12:1-2, NKJV

Elisha's preparation made way for the call of God upon him and helped him to be effective in fulfilling it. We cannot expect to wait until the moment of our call to begin our preparation. Instead, we must anticipate our calling and eagerly move forward with the divine expectation. If we are to be true spiritual sons, then we must begin now to develop a Godly work ethic, drive away hindrances, and show loyalty while we actively wait for our spiritual father to choose us.

THE ELISHA WAY

Chapter 6

THE MANTLE OF A TRUE SPIRITUAL SON

When the qualifications of a true spiritual son have been met, then the mantle of sonship can be placed. This is exactly what happened in the life of Elisha. As he had labored in his field and in his community, his hard work paid off in the form of the receipt of Elijah's mantle. After working diligently, laying aside the distractions, recognizing those who had poured into his life, and embracing a life of self-sacrifice, Elisha was rewarded with a legitimate call of God, and he became one of the most respected prophetic figures in the land.

Preparation was complete and proclamation was at hand. However, there was little Elisha could do to determine the nature of his call. God had commissioned Elijah to anoint Elisha as prophet in his place. When Elijah threw his mantle on Elisha, he was effectively calling him to take his place. Whether or not this was the calling that Elisha had desired, it was the one that God had ordained for him.

Embracing the Right Mantle

Today, we desire to see the power of God manifest in our lives. When we consider the results of Elisha embracing his calling, we recognize the value associated with accepting the mantle that God has for us. Scripture does not indicate that Elisha's calling was the one he had been waiting for. What we do find is that when Elisha embraced the call that God chose to place upon him, the power of God came.

Stephen provides a New Testament example of how this principle operates.

> *Now in those days, when the number of the disciples was multiplying, there arose a complaint against the Hebrews by the Hellenists, because their widows were neglected in the daily distribution. Then the twelve summoned the multitude of the disciples and said, "It is not desirable that we should leave the word of God and serve tables. Therefore, brethren, seek out from among you seven men of good reputation, full of the Holy Spirit and wisdom, whom we may appoint over this business; but we will give ourselves continually to prayer and to the ministry of the word." And the saying pleased the whole multitude. And they chose Stephen, a man full of faith and the Holy Spirit, and Philip, Prochorus, Nicanor, Timon, Parmenas, and Nicolas, a proselyte from Antioch, whom they set before the apostles; and when they had*

prayed, they laid hands on them. <u>*Then the*</u>
<u>*word of God spread, and the number of the*</u>
<u>*disciples multiplied greatly in Jerusalem,*</u>
and a great many of the priests were
obedient to the faith.

-Acts 6:1-7, NKJV

Examine this passage as though it were a help-wanted advertisement and consider how few present day Christians would respond with a desire for this position. While the passage makes it clear that everyone agreed that the tables should be served and that the widows should be cared for, the attitude beyond this was probably much like what would be encountered today. Everyone wanted the job to be done, but by someone else. However, the word of God indicates that there was a man present in the group, a man full of faith and the Holy Spirit, a man who was willing to accept the call of God rather than to dictate what it should be. Stephen, among six other men, was willing to embrace the mantle that was assigned to him. In so doing, he allowed himself to become a conduit of the power and anointing of God.

Stephen embraced the mantle set before him, even though it seemed to be of little value by our contemporary spiritual standards. He humbled himself and became a willing servant. The power of God is poured out because of Stephen's readiness to make himself a willing sacrifice.

> *And Stephen, full of faith and power, did*
> *great wonders and signs among the people.*
> -Acts 6:8, NKJV

The opportunity to do miracles seems more like the job description that everyone is seeking, but they arose from the mundane tasks of caring for the widows and waiting on tables. Although persecution fell quickly following the anointing in Stephen's life, he had an opportunity that many of us would pay almost any price to receive. Even in the face of opposition, he caught a glimpse into the eternal realm of heaven.

> *When they heard these things they were*
> *cut to the heart, and they gnashed at him*
> *with their teeth. But he, being full of the*
> *Holy Spirit, gazed into heaven and saw the*
> *glory of God, and Jesus standing at the*
> *right hand of God, and said, "Look! I see*
> *the heavens opened and the Son of Man*
> *standing at the right hand of God!"*
> -Acts 7:54-56, NKJV

Imagine how easily Stephen could have missed this amazing opportunity. If he had expressed the same objections to his calling that are common in the church today, he might have passed up the chance to be a servant and missed the signs, wonders, and visions that followed.

Rejecting the Wrong Mantle

If embracing God's mantle is the key to our sonship, then we must not be satisfied with any other anointing. It is amazing how many of us are so eager to receive our calling that we are willing to settle for any old piece of cloth tossed our way. We don't consider where it comes from or what impact it will have on us. We can get so caught up in the glamour of recognition that we willingly accept mantles that are not our own. Preparation to receive God's call mandates personal discernment.

One of the enemy's goals is to make us ineffective and destroy our witness. Satan knows our nature and attempts to distract us with pseudo callings that seem exciting, but belong to someone else. He tempts us with the quick path to success and offers spiritually deficient opportunities to satisfy our fleshly desires for reputation, fame, and fortune.

Quick and easy pathways rarely lead to the anticipated success. Culturally one would say, "there is no such thing as a free lunch." There will always be a cost, and the cost makes the reward worth it. The writer of the Proverbs puts it this way.

An inheritance gained hastily at the beginning will not be blessed at the end.
                    -Proverbs 20:21, NKJV

It is as essential that we reject mantles that are not our own. We find an Old Testament example of embracing an inappropriate mantle in a most unusual story. Shortly after the destruction of Jericho, the Israelites faced a devastating defeat brought about by one man's poor decision to take something that was not his own. God has provided specific directions regarding the spoils of war at Jericho.

> *And you, by all means abstain from the accursed things, lest you become accursed when you take of the accursed things, and make the camp of Israel a curse, and trouble it. But all the silver and gold, and vessels of bronze and iron, are consecrated to the LORD; they shall come into the treasury of the LORD.*
> -Joshua 6:18-19, NKJV

God mandated that the spoils be consecrated unto Him. Nevertheless, Achan chose to ignore this admonition and brought a curse upon himself as well as all the Israelites.

> *But the children of Israel committed a trespass regarding the accursed things, for Achan the son of Carmi, the son of Zabdi, the son of Zerah, of the tribe of Judah, took of the accursed things; so the anger of the LORD burned against the children of Israel.*
> -Joshua 7:1, NKJV

As a result of this one man's decision, thirty-six men lost their lives in the next battle. While this number may seem small when we consider the general consequences of war, we must remember that deaths in battle were very uncommon for the Israelites at this time. The Lord had fought every battle for His people up until this point, and none of His people had lost their life. Therefore, when thirty-six men died in one battle, the Israelites knew that something was amiss. Joshua made an immediate inquiry to discover the problem.

> *So Joshua rose early in the morning and brought Israel by their tribes, and the tribe of Judah was taken. He brought the clan of Judah, and he took the family of the Zarhites; and he brought the family of the Zarhites man by man, and Zabdi was taken. Then he brought his household man by man, and Achan the son of Carmi, the son of Zabdi, the son of Zerah, of the tribe of Judah, was taken.*
>
> *Now Joshua said to Achan, "My son, I beg you, give glory to the LORD God of Israel, and make confession to Him, and tell me now what you have done; do not hide it from me."*
>
> *And Achan answered Joshua and said, "Indeed I have sinned against the LORD God of Israel, and this is what I have done: When I saw among the spoils a beautiful Babylonian garment, two hundred shekels of silver, and a wedge of gold weighing fifty shekels, I coveted them and took them. And there they are, hidden in the earth in the midst of my tent, with the silver under it."*
>
> -Joshua 7:16-21, NKJV

Notice what Achan took from the spoils of Jericho –silver, gold, *and* a beautiful Babylonian garment. The word translated as garment is the Hebrew word *addereth* (ad-deh'-reth), which literally means something ample (as in a wide dress or a large vine) and can also be translated as mantle.[10] It is this same word translated as mantle in both 1 Kings 19:19 (where Elijah throws his mantle on Elisha) and in 2 Kings 2:14 (where Elisha takes the mantle of Elijah as it falls from him). Because the mantle of Elijah is associated with his anointing from God and is used in conjunction with the performance of several miracles, it would seem, metaphorically speaking, that Achan may have been attempting to walk in an anointing not bestowed by God. Just as it was sin for Achan to take the garment that the Lord had prohibited, it would be sin that for someone to undertake a calling not decreed by God.

Achan's sin maimed the entire camp and resulted in the death of his family. Likewise, any attempt we make to walk in a call or anointing not established by God endangers those around us. We must be careful to reject callings not designed by God.

---

[10]Biblesoft's New Exhaustive Strong's Numbers and Concordance with Expanded Greek-Hebrew Dictionary. Copyright © 1994, 2003, 2006 Biblesoft, Inc. and International Bible Translators, Inc.

Nothing can substitute for the mantle that God has for us. If we are to obtain the mantle as true sons, we must put aside our own selfish desires and wait for the Lord to settle upon us with His anointing. In addition, we must embrace the call that we receive, no matter what we think about its nature and reject false mantles, no matter how alluring they may appear.

Chapter 7
THE DEEDS OF A TRUE SPIRITUAL SON

The deeds of a true spiritual son are a valuable asset to the Kingdom of God. Both as a disciple, and then standing on his own, Elisha exemplified the actions expected from one who truly learned to follow the Father. In the church today, there are too many pew warmers and too few Word doers. The church has been long on expectation and short on results. However, as spiritual sons emerge in these end times, the church teeters on the brink of a dramatic transformation.

The deeds of true sons will bring about an explosion of spiritual activity that may stun the church and will astonish the world. The five-fold ministry outlined by Paul in Ephesians 4 is now beginning to mature, and as it does, the fullness of that passage must come to fruition. Much of the church has grown familiar (perhaps too familiar) with the members of this five-fold ministry team: apostles, prophets, evangelists, pastors, and teachers (Ephesians 4:11), but it is only now that the church is beginning to understand the true function of these ministries.

> *And He Himself gave some to be apostles, some prophets, some evangelists, and some pastors and teachers, for the equipping of the saints for the work of ministry, for the edifying of the body of Christ, till we all come to the unity of the faith and of the knowledge of the Son of God, to a perfect man, to the measure of the stature of the fullness of Christ; that we should no longer be children, tossed to and fro and carried about with every wind of doctrine, by the trickery of men, in the cunning craftiness of deceitful plotting, but, speaking the truth in love, may grow up in all things into Him who is the head -- Christ -- from whom the whole body, joined and knit together by what every joint supplies, according to the effective working by which every part does its share, causes growth of the body for the edifying of itself in love.*
> -Ephesians 4:11-16, NKJV

Notice that this passage identifies the offices and makes clear their purpose. These five types of leaders were expected to equip the saints. In other words, the spiritual fathers were supposed to train the spiritual sons according to their gifting. They were to prepare the spiritual sons for a specific intention – the work of the ministry.

Learn to Eat

We certainly understand the natural principle that we must eat in order to sustain our life, but it would appear that in much of the church today, we have forgotten this is also a valid spiritual principle. In 2 Thessalonians 3:10-12, Paul plainly states that those who do not work do not eat. He further asserts that those who prefer to meddle in everyone else's affairs and never take any initiative to act on their own are not entitled to partake of the other people's bread. This seems to indicate that if we are too busy worrying about what everyone else is doing, then it is difficult for us to accomplish our own work and that since we are not entitled to another's bread, we may at times find ourselves hungry.

The lessons taught by our spiritual fathers are described in the word of God as spiritual food.

For though by this time you ought to be teachers, you need someone to teach you again the first principles of the oracles of God; and you have come to need milk and not solid food. For everyone who partakes only of milk is unskilled in the word of righteousness, for he is a babe. But solid food belongs to those who are of full age, that is, those who by reason of use have their senses exercised to discern both good and evil.
                              -Hebrews 5:12-14, NKJV

The first or elementary principles of God are equated to milk as a source of nourishment. We are encouraged to receive this milk so that our spiritual bodies may grow strong enough to accept solid food. Notice that those who are capable of eating this solid food have exercised discernment of good and evil. While it is true that in 2 Thessalonians, Paul is clearly speaking of physical work and physical food, this passage from Hebrews helps us to see how we can take this natural principle and apply it to spiritual things. James makes this same point in a very direct way.

> *But be doers of the word, and not hearers only, deceiving yourselves. For if anyone is a hearer of the word and not a doer, he is like a man observing his natural face in a mirror; for he observes himself, goes away, and immediately forgets what kind of man he was. But he who looks into the perfect law of liberty and continues in it, and is not a forgetful hearer but a doer of the work, this one will be blessed in what he does.*
> -James 1:22-25, NKJV

> *For as the body without the spirit is dead, so faith without works is dead also.*
> -James 2:26, NKJV

Paul's admonition in 2 Thessalonians along with these passages from James provide valuable insight into why many churches today are drying up and dying from within. If spiritual sons refuse to learn and use the principles of a strong work ethic, there will be grave consequences.

Eat to Work

Ministry is work, and we all have a job to do. We have a great commission to spread the gospel of Jesus and to make disciples. No, we all can't be missionaries or preachers. However, there are many other jobs to go with our assignment. Some examples include serving in the church's food pantry, visiting shut-ins, sweeping the church after services, etc.

Simply put: sitting in a pew and listening to a sermon once or twice a week does not fulfill our mandate. Our failure to recognize our responsibility in God's Kingdom starves the church, and such an attitude has severe consequences.

Failure to engage in ministry work leads to a sort of spiritual eating disorder. We may find ourselves inside the walls of a church every time the doors are open and claim to be eating from the spiritual food served by the preacher; however, we may actually never allow our bodies the opportunity to be spiritual nourished by using (and therefore acting on) the word we received. We must not treat spiritual food as a bulimic would treat natural food. People with bulimia eat a wonderful meal and enjoy both the food and the fellowship of the mealtime, but then shortly after finishing, they vomit everything they consumed.

The same is true for spiritual bulimics who attend a church service, take of the bread of God, and then throw up what they received and go on about their busy life with absolutely no change and no recognition that their idleness causes them to wither and die.

When sons embrace the idea of the work of the ministry, they are able to eat the spiritual food presented to them and thereby grow strong, fulfilling the latter half of the Ephesians 4 passage. When sons work and thereby both eat and receive the nourishment of what they have eaten, they begin to leave childhood, where they are tossed to and fro, and grow up in all things into Him – Christ (Ephesians 4:14-15). Such growth not only benefits us as sons, but it also has deep and lasting impact upon the world around us.

Work to Grow and Produce

As children, we spend our time learning and playing. As we grow older and more mature as sons, we continue to spend our time learning and playing, but we also begin to spend an increasing amount of time working. The word translated as work in both Ephesians 4:12 (*ergon*) and in 2 Thessalonians 3:10 (*ergazomai*, the middle voice of *ergon*) can effectively be defined as "to toil as at a task or occupation".[11]As we grow from childhood to maturity, there comes a day when we must get a job of our own and stop leaning on parents to do our work for us.

Many churches today expect the fathers to do all the work of the ministry, when in reality, it should be the spiritual sons doing the work as taught by their spiritual fathers. Sad but true, pastors are resigning every day because they can't handle the pressures of being everything: an administrator, a counselor, a hospital visitor, a funeral preacher, a problem solver, an answer giver, a deep and thoughtful teacher, a wedding planner, a perfect example, a program creator, a chairman for every committee, a lone-ranger of evangelism, a visitor of every guest, etc. This type of expectation has led to one of the highest rates of pastoral burnout in the history of the church, and yet congregations are still crying out "Why?"

A pastor is to be one of the spiritual fathers and to be a good shepherd for the flock. Although it is his job to lead the sheep, it is *our* responsibility as the sheep to produce the fleece. We have a job too. Jesus, as our perfect example of a good shepherd, admonished us with the following words.

---

[11]Biblesoft's New Exhaustive Strong's Numbers and Concordance with Expanded Greek-Hebrew Dictionary. Copyright (c) 1994, Biblesoft and International Bible Translators, Inc.

"Most assuredly, I say to you, he who believes in Me, the works that I do he will do also; and greater works than these he will do, because I go to My Father.
                    —John 14:12-13, NKJV

Jesus did awesome works. He raised the dead, healed the sick, cleansed the leper, opened the eyes of the blind and the ears of the deaf. He cast out demons, made the lame to walk and the dumb to speak. He walked on water and commanded winds and waves to cease their fury. He spoke words of prophecy, prayed with passion, and taught with authority. It is these works and even greater ones that we are to do too.

Elisha began his sonship accustomed to hard work. When Elijah found him, he was out plowing in the field. This image invokes the idea that from the beginning Elisha was not just a son, but also one who would work hard as a laborer in the harvest. We live in a day in which the harvest is plentiful, but the laborers are few (Matthew 9:37). The metaphors associated with the call of Elisha make it abundantly clear that true spiritual sons are those who will take up the challenge and become laborers in the field.

We have virtually no information on what Elisha did as a part of his spiritual labor while Elijah was alive. We do know that he not only acted as a good son, but also as a true servant. Combined with the work ethic present at his calling, this aspect of Elisha's character reminds us that he was committed to do the work of the ministry. We would not see the great works done at the hand of Elisha if he had he not been practicing and preparing as he trained under Elijah.

For some time after Elijah was taken, Elisha continued to be known as the servant of Elijah. This was no doubt a compliment for a man who had labored diligently and aided his master in accomplishing the work of the ministry. In the third chapter of 2 Kings we find a story recounted regarding the kings of Israel, Judah, and Edom going to battle against the king of Moab. After some time, the king of Israel laments because it appears that God has called them together to deliver them into the hand of Moab. The king of Judah sets his mind to seek the Word of the Lord instead.

> But Jehoshaphat said, "Is there no prophet of the LORD here, that we may inquire of the LORD by him?" So one of the servants of the king of Israel answered and said, "Elisha the son of Shaphat is here, who poured water on the hands of Elijah."
> -2 Kings 3:11, NKJV

Servant / Armor-bearer

While this story itself is amazing, it is the description of Elisha that provides insight into this present topic. Notice that Elisha is identified as the one "who poured water on the hands of Elijah." This description paints a picture of Elisha as a servant.

Having traveled in many parts of the world, including East Africa (where this practice is common),

I am familiar with what it means to pour water on another's hands. It is customary prior to a meal for someone to bring a pitcher of water and a bowl and present them for those who will be eating. The one who brings the water and pours it over the hands of the guest exemplifies the lifestyle of a servant. This action illustrates an attitude of the heart by which one has great concern to see that the needs of another are met. No one has to call for the water when someone with a servant's heart is present, but rather those with this Godly character will quickly act to meet the need. Elisha was remembered in this way. He was the one with a servant's heart who didn't have to be asked to serve, but rather was quick to take up the task and pour the water on his masters hands.

In the Western culture today, if something needs to be done, the attitude seems to be that should be hired to do it. True spiritual sons are those who do not wait to be hired, paid, or even asked. Such sons are always watching for an opportunity and when they see a task they set their hands to do it. They are watching and waiting for the opportunity to pour water on the hands of another.

If we are to become true spiritual sons, we must recognize and engage in the actions associated with a servant's heart. Elisha began as a servant and became a worker of miracles. Stephen began as a waiter of tables and became a seer of the heavenly realms. What we sow in the natural we will reap in the supernatural. It is time that true spiritual sons arise and bring to an end the grumbling and complaining that runs rampant in the church. It is amazing how many people respond to a need by complaining instead of setting themselves to the task of meeting the need.

Unaddressed tasks indicate the spiritual sensitivity of the church. For every task that needs to be accomplished (whether natural or supernatural) God has issued a call for someone to do it. A dear prophetic friend of mine once said, "Cleaning the bathrooms or raising the dead, the pay is the same as long as we are doing what God has told us to do". After all, Jesus who spoke in the parable of the talents to admonish us that the one who is faithful over a few things will be made ruler over many (Matthew 25:14-30).

Chapter 8
THE CHALLENGES OF SONSHIP

The road to spiritual sonship is not an easy one. It is fraught with hardships and challenges, which can at times seem overwhelming. Folks might expect the road to grow easy once they are deemed worthy of a calling. Unfortunately, there is no principle in the Word of God to support this concept. In fact, the Word suggests that our calling is the easiest part of the process.

The Challenge of Training

Our journey begins when our Elijahs pass by and toss their mantles onto our shoulders. Just as the call to salvation is the beginning of a life-long journey of continuous growth, the call to discipleship encompasses continuous training and equipping. This training and equipping will ultimately result in our being "sent out", just as Jesus sent out His disciples. However, as with the disciples of old, the learning process does not end, but simply takes us to even higher levels of action.

97

Our spiritual training can be equated to the process a professional athlete undergoes to reach the height of their chosen sport. The effort required to reach such a state of excellence does not end when the young athlete is identified as having potential. After months and perhaps years of training the athlete may be accepted into the professional ranks; however, even then, the challenges do not stop. Likewise, true spiritual sons must continue to embrace their training.

Numerous challenges are presented for those who would continue their journey of sonship. These challenges tend to be the basis by which God tests the level of maturity that we have obtained and determines to what degree He can release us to walk in the next level of authority that He desires to give us. Elisha provides a prime example of the challenges that a spiritual son may face and the opportunities for growth that they provide.

The Challenge of Acceptability

Although Elisha clearly recognized what God did for him and understood the new authority he had following Elijah's departure, those around him didn't seem to accept the change. While they clearly recognized that the spirit of Elijah rested on Elisha (2 Kings 2:15), they did not seem to recognize that Elisha actually knew what he was talking about. In fact the sons of the prophets pressed so hard in their disbelief of what Elisha described to them, that he eventually relented and allowed them to go and search for Elijah (2 Kings 2:16-18). As we assume our spiritual place, we may be more sure of what God has shown to us than others in the church.

It is human nature for man to desire acceptance and legitimacy. When we know that we've heard from God, we naturally yearn for others to simply accept that we have, as well. Yet such acceptance is not always quick to come. Because we cannot demand acceptance, our only recourse is to allow God to touch the hearts of men and women. Elisha was patient and waited for God to establish favor on his behalf. This patience allowed others time to see that the spirit of Elijah resting on him and that the God of Elijah was working through him.

The Challenge of Humility

Elisha faced challenges within the religious community where the sons of the prophets questioned him, and challenges within the secular community where his title was yet unproven. The kings of Israel and Judah found themselves in a difficult situation, and the King of Judah asked for a prophet by whom they might inquire of the Lord (2 Kings 3:11). Instead of acknowledging Elisha as the new prophet of Israel, the group continued to refer to Elisha in reference to Elijah.

> *But Jehoshaphat said, "Is there no prophet of the LORD here, that we may inquire of the LORD by him?"*
> *So one of the servants of the king of Israel answered and said, "Elisha the son of Shaphat is here, who poured water on the hands of Elijah."*
>
> -2 Kings 3:11, NKJV

Though the world might have seen him as merely a glorified servant of a formerly great man of God, Elisha was not concerned with recognition as much as he was with fulfilling his duty before God. In fact, there is no indication in scripture that Elisha ever saw himself as anything more than a servant of God – first as a servant of God through his service to Elijah and later as a servant of God through his service to Israel and its people.

Perhaps one of the greatest challenges of true sonship is to learn to walk in the power and authority without succumbing to the snares of pride. Elisha was not one who demanded respect or titles, but rather was a true spiritual son who sought recognition of his Heavenly Father far more than man.

The best method for gaining and retaining honor is found in humility (Proverbs 29:23). Pride would have driven Elisha to seek recognition for himself, whereas humility drove him to accept whatever lot the Lord laid before him. By humbling ourselves, we allow the Lord to lift us.

*Humble yourselves in the sight of the Lord,
and He will lift you up.*
-James 4:10, NKJV

It would have been easy for Elisha to seek recognition before being willing to bring the Lord's wisdom to the situation. Instead, he accepted the title of servant. The value of such a title would have been well known by Jehoshaphat That value was acknowledge when Jehoshaphat declared, "The word of the Lord is with him," before ever even meeting Elisha(2 Kings 3:12).

The Challenge of Respectability

If we examine the story about a widow of one the sons of the prophets, we find an example of challenges associated with respectability (2 Kings 4:1-6). Here Elisha chose between assuming respectability and walking in the anointing from God. The widow's son was about to be taken as a slave to satisfy the debts her husband had left her. When Elisha appeared on the scene, the woman pleaded with him for help. In his bizarre response, he instructed her to borrow jars from all of her friends and to pour her last remaining bit of oil into all the vessels. In doing so, the woman witnessed a miracle: the oil didn't stop flowing until the supply of jars was exhausted.

No doubt, some folks initially thought Elisha's response to the widow was ridiculous. She was in debt beyond her ability, and needed immediate financial assistance. By today's standards, we would expect Elisha to take up an offering for her. Instead, with no explanation whatsoever, he instructs her to act by faith in pursuing an outrageous response to a desperate need. Elisha had a challenge to face and a choice to make. He could have pursued respectability and sought to meet her need through natural means, but instead he chose obedience in the face of potential ridicule. God's reputation and not Elisha's was on the line as a result of Elisha's act of obedience and the widow's.

A similar situation occurred in Elisha's life when Naaman requested physical healing (2 Kings 5:1-19). Naaman was an honorable man, whom even the King of Syria respected, despite the fact that Naaman was a leper. If ever there were a time for respectability, this would be it. How Elisha could have handled this encounter with the commander of the Syrian army could have an impact on the entire nation. It could have brought peace to the region, put an end to warlike raids of his people, and even brought honor and wealth to his own household, if only it were handled properly. However, once again Elisha does the unexpected. He sent a message to Naaman telling him to wash himself in the dirty Jordan River seven times. The waters of the rivers in Damascus, where Naaman was from, were clear and clean, whereas in that day the water of the Jordan River would have been turbid and colored by clay.[12]

Naaman reacted with frustration and anger. Not only had Elisha suggested he do something preposterous, but he didn't even have the courtesy to tell Naaman himself. Nevertheless, risking war with the Syrian army, Elisha chose honor for the directives of God over respect from man. He gave up any chance, by all natural standards, of receiving any earthly reward. Naaman's ultimate acceptance of this ridiculous instruction resulted in his healing.

God makes no promises that the things He asks will always make sense to us. In fact, throughout scripture, God often asked his servants to do things that made no sense to the natural mind. Spiritual sons must be willing to sacrifice their own pride and reputation to do the work of the Lord regardless of whether they understand it or not.

The Challenge of Flexibility

Spiritual sons must learn to adapt to God's timing. It can be a challenge to have our own schedule interrupted in favor of God's schedule, but the rewards

---

[12] "...the water of the Jordan is turbid, 'of a clayey colour'..." (fromKeil&Delitzsch Commentary on the Old Testament: New Updated Edition, Electronic Database. Copyright (c) 1996 by Hendrickson Publishers, Inc.)

of such interruptions can be significant. In some parts of the world, the issue of flexibility would prove to be little of a challenge, but in a time-conscious society like the United States, breaking away from a personal timetable can be a significant challenge indeed.

God desires to occupy first place on man's agenda and He will often test us to determine what position it is that we place Him in. Man thinks that the affairs of this world present the most intense challenge of flexibility; however, there is another area far more subtle. Within the mind of man, lies the idea that doing good works is the highest priority in the kingdom of God. We can easily find ourselves satisfied (and indeed pre-occupied) with well-doing that's not a part of God's agenda for us. These deeds can restrict us from seeing or doing our real tasks God has ordained. We may find ourselves bound to self-inflicted commitments and unable to act in God's timing. Elisha is a valuable example for us in handling these flexibility issues.

Elisha regularly stayed with the family of a Shunammite woman when passing through their town (2 Kings 4:8-36).One day, the woman's young boy died, and she instantly set out to find Elisha. Elisha was on Mount Carmel engaged in some kind of good work. As she approached him, she gave no indication of any trouble. But, when she reached him, she broke down and fell at his feet in desperation. Elisha must have been busy with something that he and his servant deemed important, because immediately his servant pushed away the mother.

Elisha was faced with a challenge of flexibility. Had Elisha realized that the child was dead, or had the Lord spoken to and told him that the child was dead, one might expect him to have taken the matter seriously and to have sought to help. But instead, the woman had sent word that all was well and God had hidden from him the matter at hand and he was forced to face a more challenging decision. Should he continue with his important business, or should he take time out of his schedule to listen to the woman? Elisha chose to stop what he was doing and tend to the woman. The decision to take the time and listen (not the decision to go and raise the child from the dead) is what demonstrates that Elisha chose attention to God's priorities over his own.

As spiritual sons, we will often face similar dilemmas in which we must weigh the importance of what we are doing against the circumstances arising before us. We must learn to adapt to God's timing. It can be a challenge to have our own schedule interrupted in favor of God's schedule, but the rewards of such flexibility can be significant.

The Challenge of Dependency

The challenges faced by spiritual sons will often come in forms that test our priorities in life. One who has successfully navigated the process of becoming a true spiritual son, has also come into some degree of authority. The power of God flowing through an individual can bring opportunities for financial gain. Jesus warns that money (or more particularly the love of money) can be a powerful and ungodly motivator leading individuals astray.

> *For the love of money is a root of all kinds of evil, for which some have strayed from the faith in their greediness, and pierced themselves through with many sorrows.*
> -1 Timothy 6:10, NKJV

These financial challenges may seem insignificant to those who deem themselves spiritual; however, they should by no means be taken lightly. Elisha, a well matured spiritual son, faced just such a test (2 Kings 5:1-27).

Once Naaman finally relented and dipped himself in the Jordan River, he was healed of leprosy. Naaman returned to Elisha to bless him with a gift. Elisha refused the offer. Nevertheless, his servant saw an opportunity for personal gain, hurried after Naaman, gladly accepted the gifts, and was stricken with leprosy for his actions. While Elisha had passed the test of refusing personal gain from his anointing, his servant sought wealth over God's directives and instead found himself cursed with sickness.

It is essential that a spiritual son learn to be dependent on the provision of God rather than the provision of man. This is not to say that God will never use earthly means and the hands of men to financially bless those who serve Him. The love and pursuit of money can lead to a greed that causes men to stray.

Elisha had already passed the initial test of sonship before ever facing any of these challenges. And yet, even in the midst of these challenges, Elisha was being called upon to become a spiritual father himself. While we recognize that Elisha provides unique insight into what it means to be a spiritual son, we must also understand that the challenges of sonship are intended to prepare us for a greater journey still. Spiritual sons are destined to become spiritual fathers, the foundation upon which the next generation builds. It is never too early in our journey of sonship to recognize that this perpetual growth is what God intends to bring forth, and that it is only in such growth that we will truly see the next generation of sons arise.

Chapter 9
THE REWARDS OF SONSHIP

Becoming a true spiritual son is not a task for the faint of heart, nor for those who quickly grow weary in well doing. However, the rewards associated with this path are clearly worth all of the dangers and difficulties that come with the journey. Only a fool would undertake such a journey without an understanding of the difficulties associated with it. These difficulties themselves (the very barriers that must be overcome) are the stepping-stones by which we reach the goal.

> He who overcomes shall inherit all things, and I will be his God and he shall be My son.
> -Revelation 21:7, NKJV

Ultimately, as we follow the instructions and examples of our spiritual fathers and overcome trials, we will be rewarded and called a son of the Most High. There is perhaps no greater reward than this, yet it awaits us only at the end of our journey.

So what about during our journey? Will there be intervening rewards along the way? While the answer to this question is most certainly yes, we must still act on faith by accepting the mantle and engaging in the actions of a son <u>before</u> seeing the results.

> *But without faith it is impossible to please Him, for he who comes to God must believe that He is, and that He is a rewarder of those who diligently seek Him.*
>
> -Hebrews 11:6, NKJV

We undertake the journey by faith, knowing that as we seek Him and become obedient in faith, our Father Himself will reward us.

Our Heart's Desires

In our culture today, Christians often concern themselves more with getting gifts, calls, and anointing that they desire, rather than getting those that the Lord has to give. Somehow, we seem to have confused the idea of Kingdom service with the idea of personal job we choice. Unfortunately, this could not be further from the truth and this mentality has brought division, competition, and pain to the Church. We do not have the right to do any job we choose. Obedience dictates that we function within the Kingdom in the place that God chooses. If we are to receive the true rewards of sonship, then it is essential that we begin to change our attitude and seek not our own desires, but the desires of the Father.

While the faith movement has brought many great truths to the Christian world, it has suffered abuse. Faith is a valuable asset in our pursuit of the things of God, but hyper-faith, name it and claim it teachings can become an abuse of a legitimate message. When we center our hearts on a deep and intimate relationship with the Father, He then desires to grant unto us the things that we desire. Furthermore, it is God who places those very desires in our heart in the first place. This is true with both material and spiritual things. The words of the Psalmist make this principle clear.

> *Delight yourself also in the LORD, And He*
> *shall give you the desires of your heart.*
> -Psalm 37:4, NKJV

Over the years, this passage has been twisted to teach a principle that is contrary to the Word of God. It has been misinterpreted to mean that if we will just place enough emphasis on seeking God, then He will reward us by giving us whatever we want. The context and background of this scripture help us to understand a deeper truth. A fuller reading of this passage helps us to identify just what the Psalmist intended to convey.

> *Trust in the LORD, and do good;*
> *Dwell in the land, and feed on His*
> *faithfulness.*
> *Delight yourself also in the LORD,*
> *And He shall give you the desires of your*
> *heart.*
> *Commit your way to the LORD,*

(7) Trust also in Him,
And He shall bring it to pass.
He shall bring forth your righteousness as
the light,
And your justice as the noonday.
                                    -Psalm 37:3-6, NKJV

The reward of a son is found in the relationship with God and not in what God has given him. By clearly placing the emphasis upon seeking the Lord and not upon having the desires of our heart met this passage identifies what a true spiritual son should be expecting to receive. Notice the phrases: "trust in the Lord", "do good", "feed on His faithfulness", and "commit your way". These speak of our responsibilities before the Lord. The rewards associated with fulfilling these responsibilities include bring forth our righteousness and justice. While many wish to include the idea that God will give us the desires of our heart among the rewards for our faithfulness, such a reward is not promised. Instead, this statement indicates how the Lord will bring it to pass.

The original Hebrew language makes clear that our reward is not found in having all of our personal desires handed to us on a silver platter, but rather learning to walk in righteousness and justice. In other words, as we see righteousness arise, we will begin to see holy and upright living, in accordance with God's standards[13] come forth in our lives. Furthermore, when our justice shines like the noonday, we will begin to practice what is right and just, recognizing that what is right is not only established by the standard of the law, but also by what makes for right relationships as well as harmony and peace.[14] These are the rewards for our efforts and our search. They are brought forth in us as the Lord gives us the desires of our heart.

To truly understand what is meant by giving us the desires of our heart, we must look to the underlying language. The word translated as give in Psalm 37:4 is the Hebrew word, *nathan* (naw-than'). Scholars agree that while it is possible for this Hebrew verb to mean "give" in the sense of allowing us to have something, it has an additional meaning that I believe is far more accurate in this context. It means to put, to set, to put on, to put upon, to set, to appoint, to assign, to designate.[15] Thus, it can and should be argued that this passage literally means that God will assign to us the desires of our heart, not grant us the

---

[13]Nelson's Illustrated Bible Dictionary, Copyright (c)1986, Thomas Nelson Publishers

[14]Id.

[15] The Online Bible Thayer's Greek Lexicon and Brown Driver & Briggs Hebrew Lexicon, Copyright (c)1993, Woodside Bible Fellowship, Ontario, Canada. Licensed from the Institute for Creation Research

desires of our heart. In other words, when we delight ourselves in the Lord He will assign to us the desires of our heart, so that His desires become our desires and then He can indeed grant us those desires.

By reading the passage in this way, we are able to recognize how we may have misunderstood the reception of our calling. Elisha had no more control over whose mantle was placed upon him than he did over when it would be done. It really didn't matter whether Elisha liked Elijah or if he wanted a ministry like Elijah's or not. Instead, what was important was that this was the call that God had chosen to place upon him. Elisha had fulfilled the requirements of Psalm 37 and so the Lord set in motion that which would make him into a man of righteousness and justice. The God of Heaven began to place His own heavenly desires into this earthly vessel, so that He could fulfill them through him. In the end, we see Elisha embrace this call and seek out a double portion of the anointing that Elijah had initially brought with him into that field. As a result, Elisha saw the power of God fall upon him and flow through him. This is the very thing that we cry out for today, but seem afraid to take the steps necessary to receive. Receiving such anointing requires that we give up our will and embrace the call that we receive.

A Worthy Calling

The greatest reward that we might obtain in this life is the knowledge that we have been and are walking worthy of our calling. Paul beseeched the Ephesians that they might walk in this manner:

> *I, therefore, the prisoner of the Lord, beseech you to walk worthy of the calling with which you were called, with all lowliness and gentleness, with longsuffering, bearing with one another in love, endeavoring to keep the unity of the Spirit in the bond of peace.*
> -Ephesians 4:1-3, NKJV

When we walk worthy of our calling, the desire for personal benefit seems to slip away in favor of an interest in seeing the lives of those around us changed. Paul admonishes us to take action in this life and not in the context of a coming heavenly home. In Matthew 25, Jesus presented the Parable of the Talents and expressed the concept that when we have been faithful over a few things we would hear the Master say, "Well done." There is nothing in this life that could exceed the reward that comes from knowing that Jesus acknowledges our walk to be worthy of our calling. While some may argue that such a reward cannot be attained in this life, I would suggest that we consider the fact that in the Lord's Prayer, Jesus admonishes us to pray, "...Your Kingdom come, Your will be done on earth as it is in heaven..." (Matthew

6:10). The Kingdom of Heaven can be seen here in this life. The Parable of the Talents is a parable that describes the Kingdom of Heaven, so the real question becomes "when do we expect to be commended for our walk?" While I am by no means suggesting that walking worthy of our calling is simple, I do fully believe that our obedience can be and is acknowledged as a present day reward for our sonship.

Fruit of the Spirit

Lowliness, gentleness, longsuffering, and the like are contrary to our human nature. The ability to walk in such character is most assuredly a reward bestowed from our Heavenly Father. This is the most natural of rewards, and yet if taken lightly, can seem so insignificant.

When a planted apple seed receives the right combination of elements, it will eventually sprout and grow into a sapling. Despite the challenges of wind, snow, floods, drought, and even lightning, the roots continue diving into the soil and drawing water and nutrients. The progression from a seedling to full stature takes years, after which, through no effort of its own, the tree will one day blossom and give forth fruit. That single seed from an old apple core now possesses the ability to produce apples and many more seeds of its own. Although a natural process, this cycle clearly demonstrates God's reward system.

It is also quite clearly a reward that is brought forth by God out of the tree itself.

This analogy allows us to recognize several of the rewards that are obtainable as we progress down the pathway of sonship. First and perhaps most recognizable is the fact that those who learn to walk as true spiritual sons will eventually mature and produce fruit. While the fruit produced in our lives may not look like apples or cherries, it is equally sweet. Paul reminds us in the book of Galatians that we are to bear fruit in our lives.

> But the fruit of the Spirit is love, joy, peace, longsuffering, kindness, goodness, faithfulness, gentleness, self-control. Against such there is no law.
> -Galatians 5:22-23, NKJV

This fruit bears a striking resemblance to that which Paul tells the Ephesians is necessary for us to walk worthy of our calling. In fact, several correspond rather nicely.

Ephesians 4:1-3	Galatians 5:22-23
• Lowliness	• Kindness (Meekness)
• Gentleness	• Gentleness
• Longsuffering	• Longsuffering
• Bearing with one another	• Self-Control
• In Love	• Love
• Endeavoring to Keep Unity of Spirit	• Faithfulness
• Bond of Peace	• Peace

Thus, it is the fruit of the spirit that can clearly be seen as one of the rewards of true spiritual sonship. When we consider this matter more closely it seems to be a very natural process. Just as the fruit is produced by a mature tree and shows forth the character and nature of the tree (apple trees produce apples not grapes), so the fruit of the spirit is brought forth from a mature son and shows for the character and nature of what (or in this case who) is within. For those who endure the road to spiritual sonship, they are rewarded with by the production of fruit, thus allowing the character of Christ to shine forth from within us. We exhibit this character not only for our own benefit, but so that others may see Christ's nature in us.

There is also a secondary reward that results from this process. While it is true that we can bear the character of Christ just as the tree bears fruit, we

118

must also recognize that the fruit produced by the t.ᴖe also serves an additional purpose. If we began our journey toward becoming a true spiritual son, just as the seed began its journey toward becoming a tree, then we can expect to bear of the fruit of the spirit with some of the same consequences that the bearing of natural fruit has. Among other things, when a tree produces fruit, at the very heart of that fruit, it also produces seed. These seeds, when properly planted and cared for, will produce more trees, which in turn produce more fruit. Thus, the Genesis cycle of reproduction after its own kind is carried on. As we journey toward maturity in the process of becoming spiritual sons, we will ultimately bear the fruit of the spirit. At the heart of this fruit, buried deep within us is the seed that will allow the spiritual cycle of reproduction after our own kind to be fulfilled. In this way, spiritual sons are rewarded with the ability to become spiritual fathers, who in turn can produce more spiritual sons.

Reaching this place of fruitfulness has other beneficial byproducts that could also be considered to be rewards as well. Paul wrote to the Colossians regarding his prayers for them that they might walk worthy of the Lord and become fruitful.

> For this reason we also, since the day we heard it, do not cease to pray for you, and to ask that you may be filled with the knowledge of His will in all wisdom and

We Most Constantly Seek a deeper Relationship (handwritten, left margin)

> *spiritual understanding; that you may walk*
> *worthy of the Lord, fully pleasing Him,*
> *being fruitful in every good work and*
> *increasing in the knowledge of God;*
> -Colossians 1:9-10, NKJV

Notice what it is that Paul prays. If we are to become fruitful and walk worthy of the Lord, then we must be filled with the knowledge of His will and the wisdom and spiritual understanding to walk in it. Who among us would not consider it an awesome reward to be able to know the will of God for our lives, and not only that but to have the wisdom and understanding to walk therein?

Certainly, those who would seek that place of true spiritual sonship must necessarily gain this understanding as a part of the journey. It would appear that in order to bear fruit that we must also be obedient to the will of God and in order for us to be obedient to that will, we must know that will.

When the lessons of the preceding chapters have been learned, it will not be rewards that we are seeking, but rather it will be deeper relationship that we are seeking. In that vein, as we become more diligent seekers (Hebrews 11:6) and thus begin to delight ourselves more fully in Him (Psalm 37:4), the rewards that we find along the way will be those things that enable us to more readily fulfill His plans. Rewards that come from God will, by necessity, be greater than our earthly spiritual fathers are able to give. The praise of man is of little value to a true spiritual son, however, the acknowledgment of God that we have walked worthy of the call is worth more than all the riches of the earth.

Obtaining Our Rewards

What awesome rewards indeed await those who would become spiritual sons. To live a fruitful life and to know the will of God are goals that every believer should strongly desire. Yet, on the journey to true spiritual sonship, it is essential we recognize that rewards aren't simply dropped into our lap. They must be pursued. The quest to obtain them is a valid part of our journey, and if we're not looking for such rewards, it can be easy to pass them by and never recognize that they were within our grasp.

The Apostle James reminds us that warfare is a foundational part of obtaining these rewards.

Where do wars and fights come from among you? Do they not come from your desires for pleasure that war in your members? You lust and do not have. You murder and covet and cannot obtain. You fight and war. Yet you do not have because you do not ask. You ask and do not receive, because you ask amiss, that you may spend it on your pleasures. Adulterers and adulteresses! Do you not know that friendship with the world is enmity with God? Whoever therefore wants to be a

> *friend of the world makes himself an enemy of God. Or do you think that the Scripture says in vain, "The Spirit who dwells in us yearns jealously"?*
>
> *-James 4:1-5, NKJV*

The words of James remind us that we are in the midst of a battle. We lust and covet, fight and war, but often these battles are for things that have little or no eternal value. All too frequently, we become so caught up in the affairs of this life that the spiritual things we long for are forgotten and our requests for God to give them to us are never made. When we do stop to seek His will, it takes the form of a request designed to obtain what we ourselves desire rather than what He desires. Yet, the principle remains: if we do not ask we will never have.

Elisha recognized this principle, and when the time of his spiritual maturity came, he exercised it rightly. With Solomon-like wisdom, Elisha holds his request until the timing of God is right and then unashamedly asks so that it might be fulfilled.

> *And so it was, when they had crossed over, that Elijah said to Elisha, "Ask! What may I do for you, before I am taken away from you?"*
> *Elisha said, "Please let a double portion of your spirit be upon me."*
> *So he said, "You have asked a hard thing. Nevertheless, if you see me when I am taken from you, it shall be so for you; but if*

not, it shall not be so." Then it happened, as they continued on and talked, that suddenly a chariot of fire appeared with horses of fire, and separated the two of them; and Elijah went up by a whirlwind into heaven.

And Elisha saw it, and he cried out, "My father, my father, the chariot of Israel and its horsemen!" So he saw him no more. And he took hold of his own clothes and tore them into two pieces. He also took up the mantle of Elijah that had fallen from him, and went back and stood by the bank of the Jordan. Then he took the mantle of Elijah that had fallen from him, and struck the water, and said, "Where is the LORD God of Elijah?" And when he also had struck the water, it was divided this way and that; and Elisha crossed over.

-2 Kings 2:9-14, NKJV

Elisha knew better than to judge his own maturity level. He waited on his spiritual father to offer, and when the proposal was made, he was ready to ask for what he wanted. After a long journey toward spiritual sonship and years of service, Elisha was about to reap the rewards, and his request was found to be pleasing to the Lord.

Elijah acknowledged Elisha's petition, and reminded him that it was not his to give. In addition, Elijah gives us a clue about how difficult it can be to obtain the rewards that the Lord has prepared for us. Not only has it been necessary for Elisha to live a life

123

of humility and submission, but now on the brink of maturity, he is informed that such sacrifice is not enough. Even in this the hour of his spiritual *bar mitzvah*,[16] Elisha understood that his eyes must remain fixed and never waiver from the prize.

When it was time for Elijah to leave Elisha, a chariot of fire appeared and separated them. Nevertheless, Elisha was not distracted by the glitz and glamour of supernatural things, but rather kept his eyes firmly fixed on Elijah and watched him go to heaven in a whirlwind (2 Kings 2:11).

The appearance of a chariot and horses of fire in our midst today would certainly captivate our attention, yet Elisha never flinched. He knew the difference between what was essential and what was exciting. If we desire to obtain the rewards laid up for us as spiritual sons, it is imperative that we too discern such things.

Jesus alone is essential and our eyes must remain fixed on him. Paul urged the Corinthians to imitate him as he imitated Christ (1 Corinthians 11:1).

---

[16]The time in the life of a Jewish boy when his transition from childhood to manhood is celebrated. The term "bar" is Aramaic for "son", while the term "mitzvah" is means "commandment" in both Hebrew and Aramaic. Thus, this term is literally translated "son of the commandment". It is the time when a Jewish boy becomes responsible for keeping the commandments himself, rather than continuing to come under the covering of his father. The corresponding time in the life of a young girl is referred to as the "bat mitzvah". Source: Judaism 101, www.jewfaq.org.

This suggests that prize is Christ and no matter where we look, our eyes should never waiver from Him. If we expect to obtain our reward, such diligence is an inescapable part of the cost.

THE ELISHA WAY

Chapter 10

THE ELISHA GENERATION

The Elisha Generation will comprise individuals who are willing to pay the price for deeper relationship the God of Elijah. Sonship is much deeper than simple discipleship, and nothing comes without cost, especially spiritual sonship. Consider David's mighty men and the price they paid to serve him.

> And David said with longing, "Oh, that someone would give me a drink of the water from the well of Bethlehem, which is by the gate!" So the three mighty men broke through the camp of the Philistines, drew water from the well of Bethlehem that was by the gate, and took it and brought it to David. Nevertheless he would not drink it, but poured it out to the LORD. And he said, "Far be it from me, O LORD, that I should do this! Is this not the blood of the men who went in jeopardy of their lives?" Therefore he would not drink it.
>
> -2 Samuel 23:15-17, NKJV

This passage speaks volumes about the costs of spiritual sonship. These mighty men who served David broke through the camp of the Philistines to obtain the water for him. They did not embark on this life-threatening mission because of its value to the entire kingdom, nor did they go forth at their king's command, but rather they sought to serve the one they loved. These men risked their lives for a simple act of service for one they loved like a father.

Those who don't understand discipleship or have sought to use it for personal gain and reputation have cheapened it over the years. The next generation will not settle for this lip service. Like Elisha, once they have committed themselves to true discipleship, they will not look back. When this generation commits to the spiritual fathers (who are now arising), they will sacrifice everything and gain the double portion available to them.

Certainly, today's generations are living in the last days, and we are perhaps nearing what Malachi calls the great and dreadful day of the Lord.

> *Behold, I will send you Elijah the prophet before the coming of the great and dreadful day of the LORD. And he will turn the hearts of the fathers to the children, and the hearts of the children to their fathers, lest I come and strike the earth with a curse."*
>
> -Malachi 4:5-6, NKJV

These are also the days of Elijah – days of great trial and opportunity. We must be desperate in this hour to know the heart of our Heavenly Father. What better way for Him to reveal it, but through the restoration of spiritual fathers among us?

Additionally, this generation springing up among us wants more than just *knowing about* God. They want to *experience* Him. This generation needs an Elijah/Elisha example. They are looking for spiritual fathers who are real – who "walk the walk, instead of talk the talk". This generation will never be satisfied with a form of godliness that denies the power thereof. (2 Timothy 3:5). They cry out for their destiny and refuse a weak and powerless church that pretends to offer discipleship.

> *For the kingdom of God is not in word but in power.*
> -1 Corinthians 4:20, NKJV

In order for the church to fulfill its role and walk in the power to which it's called, the Elijahs of God must stand up and be counted. They must step forward and begin turning the hearts of this generation back to our Heavenly Father.

The generation today has the opportunity to experience the power and presence of God in a way that no other generation before them has. They are an Elisha generation, one on the brink of either obtaining or missing their double portion.

Let the Elijahs of God arise, pour their hearts into those who will take the kingdom to the next level, and possess a portion that can be doubled. Let the Elishas of God arise, take up their mantle, and walk in a double anointing.

THE ELISHA WAY

ABOUT THE AUTHOR

After practicing law for 16 years, Michael B. French received his call into the ministry. Over the past 27 years, he has passionately ministered all around the world. Michael is the director of Cahaba Equipping Center, a Streams Ministries Training Center and teaches courses such as *The Art of Hearing God* and *Understanding Dreams & Visions* for John Paul Jackson. He also serves as Director of Missions and International Church Development for The Association of Bridge Churches. Michael and his wife live in Leeds, Alabama with their four sons.

Download QR Code Reader and scan from your smart phone or visit the web addresses to enjoy Michael's links.

- **Michael's Twitter:** @revmike88

- **Michael's FaceBook:**
  http://www.facebook.com/authormichaelbfrenc
  h

THE ELISHA WAY

NOTES

CPSIA information can be obtained at www.ICGtesting.com
Printed in the USA
LVOW081249230612

287210LV00003BA/3/P